I accompany the
"100 best places to stay"
- for 2009!
Bozeley. xoxo

The Bridgestone
100 Best Restaurants in Ireland

2008 EDITION

www.bridgestoneguides.com

THE BRIDGESTONE

100 BEST RESTAURANTS IN IRELAND 2008

JOHN McKENNA - SALLY McKENNA

ESTRAGONPRESS

FIRST PUBLISHED IN NOVEMBER 2007

BY ESTRAGON PRESS

DURRUS

COUNTY CORK

ISBN - 978-1-874076-87-2

TYPESET IN GILL ALTERNATE TO

AN ORIGINAL DESIGN BY NICK CANN

ILLUSTRATIONS BY AOIFE WASSER

PRINTED IN SPAIN BY GRAPHYCEMS

• Front cover photos: bottom left, chef Tom Doyle, top left and middle right courtesy of Ely HQ.

WRITTEN & EDITED BY JOHN McKENNA

CONTRIBUTING EDITORS:

EAMON BARRETT

GILLIAN BOLTON

KARYN BOOTH

ORLA BRODERICK

CAROLINE BYRNE

SABRINA CONNEELY

ELIZABETH FIELD

CLAIRE GOODWILLIE

VALERIE O'CONNOR

LESLIE WILLIAMS

PUBLISHING EDITOR: SALLY McKENNA

EDITOR: JUDITH CASEY

EDITORIAL ASSISTANT & WEB PICTURE EDITOR: EVE CLANCY

WEB: FLUIDEDGE.IE

FOR:

Olivia Goodwillie

WITH SPECIAL THANKS TO

Des Collins, Colm Conyngham, Pat Curran, Grainne Byrne, Julie Barrett, George Lane, Frank McKevitt, Miguel Sancho, Hugh Stancliffe, Connie McKenna, Sam McKenna, PJ McKenna

Bridgestone is the world's largest tyre and rubber company.

• Founded in Japan in 1931, it currently employs over 100,000 people in Europe, Asia and America and its products are sold in more than 150 countries. Its European plants are situated in France, Spain, Italy, Poland and Turkey.

• Bridgestone manufacture tyres for a wide variety of vehicles from passenger cars and motorcycles, trucks and buses to giant earthmovers and aircraft.

• Many new cars are fitted with Bridgestone tyres during manufacture, including Ford, Toyota, Volkswagen, Mercedes and BMW. Ferrari and Porsche are also fitted with Bridgestone performance tyres as original equipment.

• Bridgestone commercial vehicle tyres enjoy a worldwide reputation for durability and its aircraft tyres are used by more than 100 airlines.

• In Formula 1 Bridgestone are sole tyre supplier with all the teams now competing on its Potenza racing tyres. Technology developed in the sport has led to increased performance and safety in Bridgestone's road tyres.

• Bridgestone tyres are distributed in Ireland by Bridgestone Ireland Ltd, a subsidiary of the multinational Bridgestone Corporation. A wide range of tyres is stocked in its 6,500 square metre central warehouse and its staff provide sales, technical and delivery services all over Ireland.

• Bridgestone tyres are available from First Stop Tyre Centres and tyre dealers throughout Ireland.

For further information:

BRIDGESTONE IRELAND LTD
10 Fingal Bay Business Park
Balbriggan
County Dublin

Tel: + 353 1 841 0000
Fax: + 353 1 841 5245

websites:
www.bridgestone.ie
www.firststop.ie

• The queer gear merchants are coming out on top. Whether it is the spicy fried dried jelly fish dish in Dublin's Green Island, or Carmel Somer's cutting-edge ham sandwich in West Cork, or the eight courses of the no-choice tasting menu of local foods at Tipperary's The Old Convent, or the smoked roe stuffed morels with turbot cutlet in Kerry's Out Of The Blue, those Irish restaurants who are pushing the boat out with local, seasonal, limited-edition, bespoke products and techniques are packing in the punters, and defining the modern Irish restaurant zeitgeist.

• A decade ago, these people would have struggled to survive. Today, they run the busiest restaurants in the country, as a new generation of inquisitive restaurant-goers flock to those chefs whose culinary signature is the most personal, the most selective, and the most seductive.

• Meantime, the rest of the Irish culinary world is braising lamb shanks and making confit belly of pork until the lambs and the pigs come home. They are losing out by offering menus that are too similar, too unseasonal, and too restricted in ambition. These restaurants are behind the desires of their customers.

• Avant garde or vanguard? There is only one place for a smart restaurant to be.

John & Sally McKenna
Durrus, West Cork, October 2007

"I discovered what it means to live within a food tradition. I learned to understand the many ways in which simplicity manifests in cooking. Ironically, simplicity represents the trouble that many generations of cooks have taken to arrive at the best expression of their native ingredients."

Paul Bertolli, *Cooking by Hand*

Paul Bertolli's beautifully aphoristic musings on the business of being a cook, in his 2003 book *Cooking by Hand,* present some of the most insightful revelations about what it means to cook seriously, as a means of exploring a tradition, and of furthering and enriching that tradition. "Authenticity has its own taste yet its principles are universal", he writes, as good a touchstone as any young chef could possibly have as they attempt to make sense of the agricultural and culinary world around and about them.

We mention the agricultural world, because "Eating is an agricultural act", in the famous words of Wendell Berry. Yet too few chefs are aware of the agricultural culture in which they live, despite the fact that their job, surely, should be to achieve the culinary simplicity that is the "best expression of their native ingredients". Yes, chefs learn their trade in schools and colleges and kitchens. But they should also be learning their trade on farms, amongst farmers. The farmer and the chef should be friends, and the chefs who take the trouble to know the culture of their agriculture will find that beautiful simplicity much quicker than those who do their learning only in kitchens.

hot

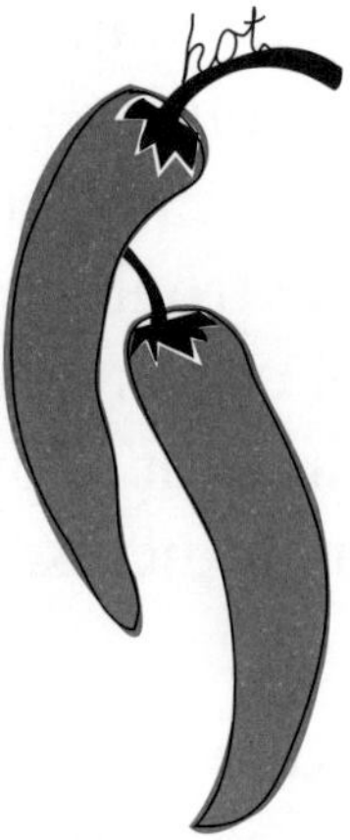

The Ballymore Inn 87
Bassett's At Woodstock 89
Chapter One 52
Ely 56
Fallon & Byrne 57
Fishy Fishy Cafe 33
Good Things Café 34
James Street South 123
L'Ecrivain 53
MacNean Restaurant 24
Mint 64
Nick's Warehouse 125
The Old Convent 101
Out Of The Blue 84
Nephin Restaurant 96
Shu 128
The Strawberry Tree 112
The Tannery Restaurant 104
The Winding Stair 75

classic

Alden's 115
Ballymaloe House 28
Brocka on the Water 98
Café Hans 99
Café Paradiso 29
Caviston's 51
The Chart House 82
Farm Gate Café 32
Longueville House 39
La Marine 109

new

• The Bridgestone 100 Best Restaurants in Ireland is arranged alphabetically, by county, so it begins with County Carlow, which is followed by County Cavan, and so on. Within the counties, the entries are once again listed alphabetically. Entries in Northern Ireland are itemised alphabetically, at the end of the book. All NI prices are quoted in sterling.

• The contents of the Bridgestone 100 Best Guides are exclusively the result of the authors' deliberations. All meals and accommodation were paid for and any offers of discounts or gifts were refused.

• Many of the places featured in this book are only open during the summer, which means that they can be closed for any given length of time between October and March.

• Prices: Dinner prices are calculated for an average three-course menu, without wine. Where the restaurant operates a set menu, that price is given.

• Listings: In every entry in the book we try to list address, telephone number, and internet details. We also request details of disabled access, plus any other relevant information.

• Websites: Where an entry has a website, we always print the address, as this is the place where you will find most up-to-date information as well as special offers. All the entries in all the Bridgestone Guides can be found on www.bridgestoneguides.com.

• Telephone Numbers: Telephone numbers are listed using the international dialling code. If you are calling a number within the country, omit the international code and use the 0.

• Bridgestone plaques: Look out for our Bridgestone Plaques, displayed by many of our listed establishments.

SHA ROE BISTRO

Henry Stone & Stephanie Barrilier
Main Street, Clonegal
County Carlow
+353 (0) 53-937 5636
sha-roebistro@hotmail.com

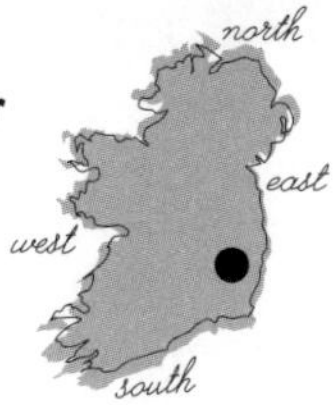

Henry and Stephanie haven't put a knife and fork wrong in quickly creating a devoted audience for beautiful cooking and great service in Sha Roe.

Things are working out nicely for Henry and Stephanie in Sha Roe, and their mixture of rusticity and slick modernism has proven itself to be just what regular customers are craving. Mixing that slickness with rustic depth in his food is just what Mr Stone does, making for eating that is light yet pleasingly unctuous – modern classics such as scallops with cauliflower purée or sardines with slow-roasted tomatoes rub shoulders with timeless comfort dishes such as rump of Wexford lamb with boulangère potatoes or guinea fowl with ham shank, peas and mash. Nice food, very nice food.

Keeping the menu restricted to half a dozen starters and half a dozen main courses means the kitchen is on top of everything, and the cooking hits full pitch at every point through the evening, from lamb kebabs with yogurt through monkfish with braised leeks and onto one of the best cheese plates featuring Knockdrinna and Lavistown from Kilkenny along with Coolattin Cheddar, Bellingham Blue and Elizabeth Bradley's fine Carlow Cheese. Sha Roe is professional and inspiring, and very fine.

- **OPEN:** 7pm-9.30pm Wed-Sat; 12.30pm-3pm Sun
- **PRICE:** Sun Lunch €30, Dinner €40
- **CREDIT CARDS:** Visa, Mastercard, Laser, Amex

- **NOTES:**

Wheelchair access, but no disabled toilet

- **DIRECTIONS:**

Just off the N80 Enniscorthy-Carlow road, 8km from Bunclody. From Wexford take the Enniscorthy-Bunclody road. From Kilkenny take the N10.

THE WATERFRONT

George Kehoe
The Lord Bagenal Hotel
Leighlinbridge, County Carlow
+353 (0) 59-972 1668
www.lordbagenal.com
info@lordbagenal.com

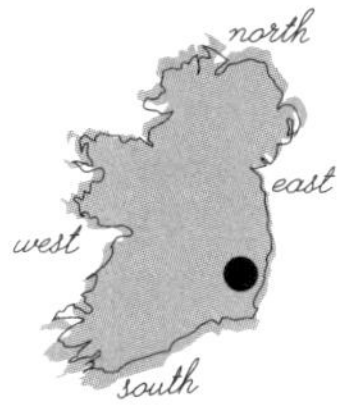

One of few restaurants where molecular cooking is shown in its glory, The Waterfront is red hot.

Molecular cooking is a rock built on difficult ground. Few cooks can pull off the grace notes that the great innovators of the cuisine intend, with the result that their foams are just froths and their savoury-sweet inversions are just a waste of energy. But, one chef who has the grace for the grace notes of modern molecular cooking is George Kehoe, and in the slick new restaurant of his Dad, James's, new hotel, he has just the space in which to show what he can do.

The savoury-sweet inversion of a horseradish ice cream proves to be a perfect foil for outsanding carpaccio of beef, whilst a lavender honey with air-dried lamb is inspired. Chickpea fries with red mullet again shows the chef getting outside the box with great success, whilst strip of veal with smoked Gubbeen and potato gratin is similarly free-thinking and successful, and pan-fried cod with roast shellfish sauce and deep-fried celery leaf is perfect. Desserts maintain the stellar standards, and just watch this chef and his crew develop as they grow in confidence and as this smart, modern cooking evolves.

● **OPEN:** 6.30pm-9.30pm Wed & Thu, 6.30pm-10pm Fri & Sat, 12.30-4.30pm Sun
● **PRICE:** Sun lunch €30, Dinner €55-€65
● **CREDIT CARDS:** Visa, Mastercard, Laser, Amex

● **NOTES:**
Full wheelchair access to restaurant and hotel.

● **DIRECTIONS:**
On the main street in Leighlinbridge, which is just off the N9 Dublin-Waterford road, an hour and a half from Dublin city centre.

MacNEAN RESTAURANT

Neven & Amelda Maguire
Blacklion
County Cavan
+353 (0) 71-985 3022
www.macneanrestaurant.com
info@macneanrestaurant.com

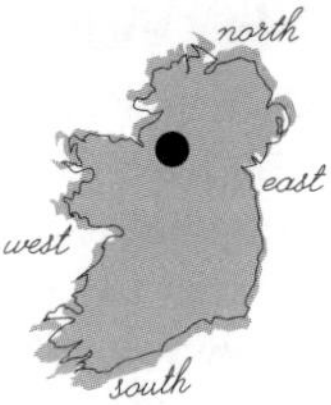

Is Neven Maguire's cooking worth a 600-kilometre drive? Mr Maguire's cooking is worth a 600-kilometre walk.

Eamon Barrett drove 300kms north to eat at the MacNean. After 299.5kms, his wheels gave up. When he finally got into the MacNean, in tiny little Blacklion, the staff said "It's a pleasure to have you here." The kitchen sent out two Kir Royale straight away. "Stress? What stress?" asks Mr Barrett. Bridgestone editors: they're tough. And, after 300kms, they are also mighty hungry, No better place to be then, than Neven and Amelda Maguire's ground-breaking restaurant. And the highlights?

"West Coast lobster plate with lobster ravioli, potato salad, sausage and coconut soup / Mosaic of quail stuffed with wild mushrooms served on a bed of pea risotto with a grape, celery and walnut salad / Amazing sautéed freshwater crayfish with linguini pasta and shellfish foam and for mains Irish lamb three ways - an outstanding dish of 2-star quality - with roast loin, braised shoulder and neck stew / Line-caught wild seabass served with borlotti beans, pasta and cep veloute. Desserts were fabulous, staff are wonderful." And 300 happy kms home.

- **OPEN:** 6pm-9pm Wed-Sun; 1pm & 3.30pm Sun (closed Wed low season). Closed Jan
- **PRICE:** Sun Lunch €35, Dinner €70-€80
- **CREDIT CARDS:** Visa, Mastercard, Laser

NOTES:
Wheelchair access. Recommended for Vegetarians, special menu. Ten guestrooms.

DIRECTIONS:
On the main street in Blacklion, which itself is just on the border with Northern Ireland.

THE OLDE POST INN

Tara McCann & Gearoid Lynch
Cloverhill, Butler's Bridge
County Cavan
+353 (0) 47-55555
www.theoldepostinn.com
gearoidlynch@eircom.net

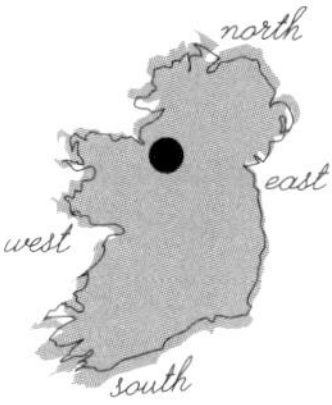

Some of the most splendidly textured – as well as splendidly tasting – cooking is the signature style in Tara and Gearoid's red hot Olde Post Inn.

Chefs pay a lot of attention to tastes, but too few of them pay attention to textures. Gearoid Lynch doesn't make this mistake. His cooking is alive to the possibility of texture – the toothy yield of beef carpaccio; the smooth embrace of potato purée; the contrast of shiitake mushroom with snipe; the altogether different and comforting yield of a bread and butter pudding – so much so you suspect – and expect – that this man could make excellent Dim Sum.

Well, he does do a superb duck won ton with cucumber salad, showing exactly how this much-maligned dish should be created, but truth be told his penchant for textures is evident in everything he cooks, from the incredibly precise texture of potato scales with turbot to the comfort of cod baked with mash to a gorgeous fig tart. Thanks to the textural qualities, the food is wonderfully enlivening, as enlivening as the superb staff. The new conservatory has added a further comfort element to a comfortable restaurant, the rooms are getting a major overhaul, and ambition is sky-high in the Olde Post.

- **OPEN:** 6.30pm-9pm Tue-Sat; 12.30pm-2.30pm, 6pm-8.30pm Sun (last orders Fri & Sat 9.30pm)
- **PRICE:** Sun Lunch €29, Dinner €56
- **CREDIT CARDS:** Visa, Mastercard, Laser, Amex

NOTES:
Wheelchair access to restaurant. Six guestrooms.

DIRECTIONS:
From Cavan follow N3. At Butler's Bridge, take the N54 and the Olde Post is 3km further, on the right.

CHERRY TREE RESTAURANT

Harry McKeogh
Lakeside, Ballina, Killaloe
County Clare
+353 (0) 61-375688
www.cherrytreerestaurant.ie

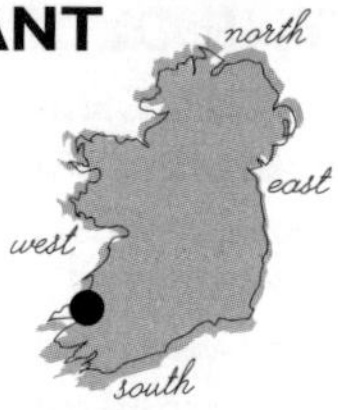

Harry McKeogh's cooking continues the line and logic of great Irish chefs like Michael Ryan and John Cooke, and it finds a lovely home in the CT.

Harry McKeogh is back in the kitchen with his apron on, after a spell moonlighting as f-of-h in his waterside restaurant. The flavour principles and flavour points which Mr McKeogh learned in great kitchens such as Arbutus in Cork and Cooke's in Dublin, with great chefs such as Michael Ryan and John Cooke, are the mainstay of his signature style: roasted scallops with saffron risotto and watercress; wild wood pigeon with chicory, apples and walnut purée; sea bass with basil linguini and sauce vierge; Angus beef with potato gratin and cabernet sauvignon jus; strudel of apple and poppy seeds with honey ice cream. This is classic food, with every pairing utterly logical, with flavour finesse balanced with a flavour fortitude that is sublimely pleasing.

But it doesn't mean that CT menus are written in stone. McKeogh can fire out a funky version of chipotle Caesar salad with jalapeno polenta crouton, or a cappuccino of smoked haddock and mussel chowder to match anyone, and the balance between the classics and the cutting-edge means that the CT is a restaurant for everyone.

- **OPEN:** 6pm-10pm Tue-Sat, 12.30pm-3pm Sun
- **PRICE:** Dinner €48, Sun Lunch €24 two courses, €29 three courses.
- **CREDIT CARDS:** Visa, Mastercard, Laser, Amex

● NOTES:

Wheelchair access. Children's menu.

● DIRECTIONS:

Drive through Ballina village, turn left towards the bridge and right at Molly's pub, towards Lakeside Hotel.

VAUGHAN'S ANCHOR INN

Denis Vaughan
Main Street
Liscannor, County Clare
+353 (0) 65-7081548
www.vaughans.ie
info@vaughans.ie

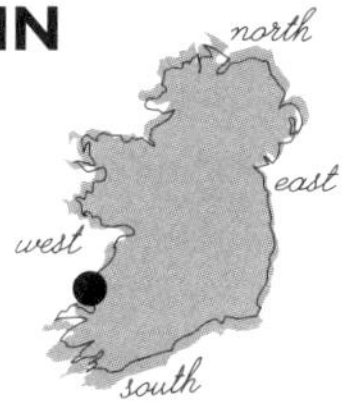

If "sighs of customer pleasure" were an index of excellence, Vaughan's is the star of the county.

Denis Vaughan's restaurant mixes a quirky old-style bar at the front, complete with coal fire, suitably distressed old banquettes and packets of biscuits for sale along with the beer, with a restaurant offer that spreads over two rooms at the rere. Here, under the ultra-professional gaze of the ultra-professional Suzanne, the ambition of the kitchen is straightaway signalled by fine glassware and a little amuse of a pork lollipop with an awesome aubergine jam. Bang! He's got you, one because you don't expect an amuse in such a simple place and, secondly, because the lollipop is the bestest lollipop you have had since you were four years old.

Sometimes they can gild the lily too much – a rarebit topping with hake and a shellfish ragout is beautifully done, but superfluous; a tempura batter with prawns could be lighter – but this cooking is involved and involving, and standards of execution are sky-high: we thought the table of Americans next to us were going to faint away with the multiple sighs of pleasure they were emitting. Mr Vaughan is still questing, so we can expect a lot.

● **OPEN:** 12.30pm-9pm Mon-Sun. Bar food daily, dinner in restaurant.
● **PRICE:** Dinner €40, Bar Lunch mains €12-€15
● **CREDIT CARDS:** Visa, Mastercard, Laser

● **NOTES**
Wheelchair access.

● **DIRECTIONS:**
In the centre of Liscannor.

BALLYMALOE HOUSE

The Allen family
Shanagarry, Midleton
East Cork
+353 (0) 21-465 2531
www.ballymaloe.ie
res@ballymaloe.ie

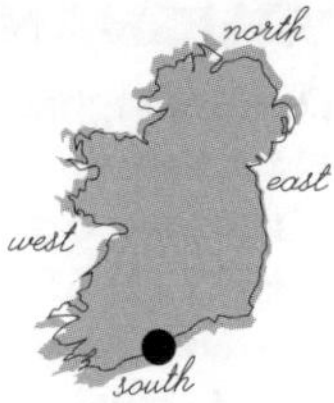

History is the great help-meet of Ballymaloe House, the destination that evokes centuries of Irish food.

"My mother's mother had lived through the Famine." When you hear Myrtle Allen say something like this, as she relayed it to a conference audience at which we were present, you understand that the time continuum in which she is working is completely, radically different from the time frame in which the rest of us are working. Such a statement explains a lot – and may also explain just how Mrs Allen is the sprightliest octogenarian we know. It explains why the concept of "fashion" is such a nonsense to Ballymaloe House. It explains why tradition here is not an affectation, but is instead a living memory, a trove of influence, a store of intellect.

It explains how Ballymaloe can seem to be both the most venerable of places, and the most up-to-date. It explains how and why the superb cooking and the peerless hospitality have such a vivid distinctiveness. Ballymaloe is cooking and hospitality as a sustainable art form, a sustainable life form, progressing through generation after generation, never atrophying but always being reborn, renewed. In Ballymaloe, history is the welcome guest.

- **OPEN:** 7pm-9pm dinner, 1pm lunch Mon-Sun
- **PRICE:** Lunch €40, Dinner €70
- **CREDIT CARDS:** Visa, Mastercard, Laser, Amex

● NOTES:

Wheelchair access with assistance. 33 guest rooms. Early children's dinner.

● DIRECTIONS:

29km east of Cork city. Take the N25 and exit for Whitegate R630, follow signs for R629 Cloyne. The House is 3km beyond Cloyne, signposted.

CAFÉ PARADISO

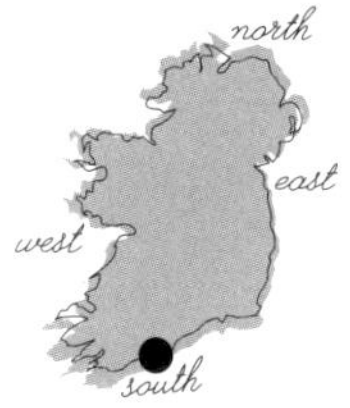

Denis Cotter
16 Lancaster Quay
Cork, County Cork
+353 (0) 21-427 7939
www.cafeparadiso.ie
info@cafeparadiso.ie

Denis Cotter's cooking doesn't explore culinary genres: it explodes them. The Banksy of the kitchen.

It is always great fun to meet someone who has just had their first ever dinner at Café Paradiso. It's fun simply because even the most loquacious food lover can suddenly find themselves tongue-tied in trying to explain the challenges and pleasures of the meat-free cooking produced by Denis Cotter and his crew. Our last encounter was with an American writer who could not have been more loquacious, or more tongue-tied. "Amazing...colourful.. never before... so different... new experience...surprise of flavours... everything unexpected... don't know where to start... amazing... nothing like it." It's a bit like talking to a three-year-old. But that is the measure of the CP experience. This food is unlike any other. There is no meat used, the room is simple, and so what arrives on the plate is even more surprising than when you read it on the menu. What will "Egg roll pancake of asparagus, Durrus cheese and sea spinach with a warm cherry tomato and avocado salsa and new season Nicola potatoes" taste like? Like nothing you have ever eaten before, is the simple answer.

- **OPEN:** noon-3pm, 6.30pm-10.30pm Tue-Sat
- **PRICE:** Lunch €20, Dinner €47
- **CREDIT CARDS:** Visa, Mastercard, Laser, Amex

- **NOTES:**

Wheelchair access, but no disabled toilet. Three guestrooms available.

- **DIRECTIONS:**

Cafe Paradiso is opposite the Lancaster Lodge, and is on your right as you head away from the city.

CASINO HOUSE

Kerrin & Michael Relja
Coolmain Bay, Kilbrittain
West Cork
+353 (0) 23-49944
chouse@eircom.net

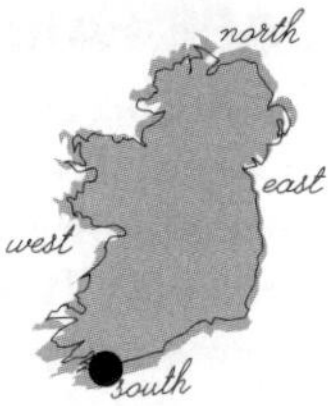

Kerrin and Michael effortlessly resolve all the contradictions of Casino House to produce a distinctive restaurant with deliciously individual cooking.

"Instead of splendour it has warmth... cool, not clinical, informal without being casual... something iconic yet familiar... mellow hints of the identity, and achievements, of Casino House."
The writer Mary Leland's apt summation of Michael and Kerrin Relja's restaurant points out the contradictions that this talented couple have managed to reconcile, seemingly with ease, as they have carved out their reputation over the last decade. Perhaps it is the fact that they hail, respectively, from Croatia and the Friesian Islands that lets them unpick so many knots with such ease, that means they see contrast where others might see contradiction. But however they have managed it, they have a classic restaurant in the West Cork style – unpredictable, funky, stylish, with very distinctive cooking – and they run it superbly. Mr Relja is a chef's cook – lots of technique, lots of prep to get him through service – but the food has beautiful grace notes – gnocchi with lemon and sage; lamb saddle with courgettes; duck with mushroom stew – and the house is just sublime.

- **OPEN:** 17 Mar-Dec, 7pm-9pm, closed Wed; weekends only Nov & Dec; open Sun lunch
- **PRICE:** Lunch €25, Dinner €45
- **CREDIT CARDS:** Visa, Mastercard, Laser, Amex

NOTES:
Wheelchair access. Gate Lodge cottage available to rent nightly/weekly €85 per night or €150 for 2 days.

DIRECTIONS:
On the R600 between Timoleague and Kinsale. Casino House is signposted from Ballinspittle.

CROOKHAVEN INN

Emma Jepson & Freddy Olsson
Crookhaven
West Cork
+353 (0) 28-35309
crookhaveninn@eircom.net

A gastropub that is just what a gastropub should be, Emma and Freddy's Inn in deepest West Cork is someplace that is quietly, sweetly special.

Emma and Freddy's sweet little bar in sweet little Crookhaven is what every gastropub should be. A place of simplicity and comfort, with switched-on service, where the food seems utterly of its time and place: smoked salmon and crab quiche; Fisherman's pie; beef and ale stew; fusilli with chicken and pesto; Bantry Bay mussels; salmon fish cakes.

This is the kind of place that makes critics redundant, because all they are doing is what they are good at doing, and that is what everyone wants them to do because that is what everyone likes. Put it that baldly, and you might think there is nothing special to the Crookhaven Inn, but you would be wrong. You can drive down the peninsula sightseeing with your mammy – as we did recently – and stop for a bowl of their superb chowder, and the correctness and comfort of the dish will make that little expedition special. And that is their secret: Low-key magic. Understated brilliance. Modest originality. It's not easy to be those things, but Emma and Freddy and their crew manage it, and West Cork is grateful.

- **OPEN:** 12.30pm-9pm Mon-Sun, low season check times. Closed Oct-St Patrick's weekend
- **PRICE:** Lunch €17, Dinner €32
- **CREDIT CARDS:** Visa, Mastercard, Laser

- **NOTES:**

Wheelchair access. (Access to male toilet only.)

- **DIRECTIONS:**

Overlooking the harbour in the centre of Crookhaven Village.

FARM GATE CAFÉ

Kay Harte
English Market
Cork, County Cork
+353 (0) 21-427 8134
farmgatecafe@yahoo.ie

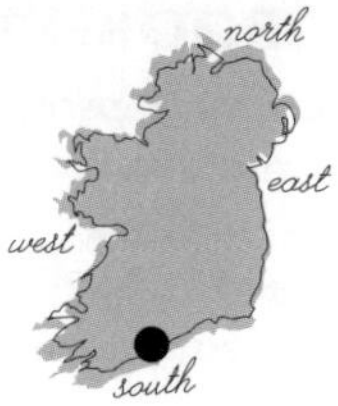

The Farm Gate is the café of the English Market, and by the English Market: symbiotic sustainability.

We had dinner recently with Ari Weinzweig, visionary founder of the world-famous Zingerman's deli in Ann Arbor, Michigan. "We have a new restaurant now," said Ari quietly. "And we only serve local food."
By that light, Kay Harte's Farm Gate would be Ari's Restaurant Made in Heaven. What you get here is not just local food, it is the food sold by the retailers downstairs in the English Market itself. The Market feeds the Farm Gate and the Farm Gate feeds the people of Cork. What logic! What deliciousness! What delicious logic!
Ms Harte is one of those mighty Cork women – her sister Marog of Midleton's Farm Gate is another – who seem carved from something other than flesh and bone: they seem to be made of pure will, with an amuse of utter determination, and a digestif of humorous culture.
"The English Market, first and foremost, is a place where Cork people can come to shop, in a wonderful environment, and be sustained by nutritious food." Cooking that sustaining food is Ms Harte's calling, and she does it superbly, traditionally, with chutzpah, and no little style.

- **OPEN:** 8.30am-5pm Mon-Sat
- **PRICE:** Lunch €10-€15
- **CREDIT CARDS:** Visa, Mastercard, Laser

NOTES:
No wheelchair access.

DIRECTIONS:
Upstairs in the centre of Cork's English Market, which runs between Patrick Street and Oliver Plunkett Street in the city centre.

FISHY FISHY CAFE

Martin & Marie Shanahan
Crowley Quay,
Kinsale, West Cork
+353 (0) 21-470 0415
www.fishyfishy.ie

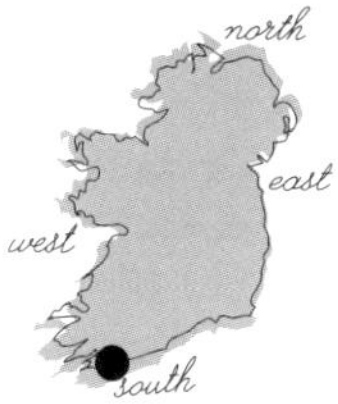

Martin and Marie Shanahan and their super slick crew are setting stellar new standards in the sublime Fishy Fishy.

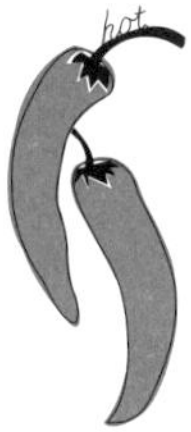

"Wonderful. Sets a new standard." That's what our regular correspondent from Northern Ireland, Mr Hanna, noted about Fishy Fishy after a summer visit. As we had a trip planned, we delayed before replying. After we got back, we wrote: "Have to agree with you: they are really setting new standards, in virtually every department, and are apparently, now they are staying open until 7-8pm, doing 350-450 covers a day. In little Kinsale! A fantastic achievement."
Regular readers might wonder just how this brilliant seafood restaurant could possibly have gotten any better, but better is just what it's gotten. The synchronicity between cooking, service, atmosphere and style is truly of a new standard. Name-check the finest restaurants in Ireland at their finest moments – Roscoff in 1991, Truffles in 1996, Chapter One in 2006, make your own star chart – and to that list you have to add Fishy Fishy Café in 2007/8. Skate wing with samphire, capers and chanterelles is a dream dish, Thai-style mussels are perfection; crispy fish with skinny chips is perfect youngster's food.

● **OPEN:** Café noon-4.30pm Mon-Sun
Open noon-8pm Tue-Fri during Jun-Sept
● **PRICE:** Lunch €35
● **CREDIT CARDS:** No credit cards

● **NOTES:**
Wheelchair access. No reservations. Fishy Fishy Shop, serving simple food and fresh fish, open noon-3.30pm Tue-SatApr-Sept +353 (0) 21-477 4453.

● **DIRECTIONS:**
On the waterfront near Acton's Hotel.

GOOD THINGS CAFÉ

Carmel Somers
Ahakista Road, Durrus
West Cork
+353 (0) 27-61426
www.thegoodthingscafe.com
info@thegoodthingscafe.com

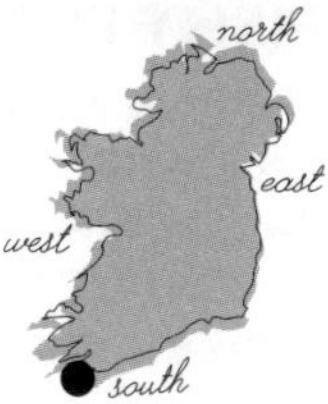

The humble ham sandwich elevated to an art form. That's the magic Carmel Somers is weaving in Good Things Café.

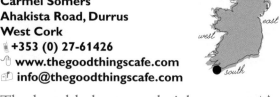

Who else would have the nerve to put "A really good ham sandwich" on their brunch menu? Well, Carmel Somers, for one, had that sandwich on the brunch menu at GTC during the season, and whilst the sarnie itself was a triumph – Gubbeen ham, Good Things bread, rich butter, tarragon mustard – it is the confidence implicit in offering such a dish that shows just how far Ms Somers has come in just four or five seasons. Good Things doesn't just offer the best cooking in West Cork: it offers some of the very best cooking in all of Ireland, cooking that speaks of inspiration and improvisation, of creativity and confidence, of signature and style, of seasonality and sourcing. From dishes such as Sugar Club beef with its immense clout of flavour to the sublime Durrus cheese, spinach and nutmeg pizza with its sovereign individuality, this cooking is like none other. Every dish seems not just hand-tooled, but also comprehensively re-thought, before being delivered with simplicity and grace by a superb team. When you can re-imagine the ham sandwich, than you are truly a star.

- **OPEN:** 11.30am-4pm (lunch served from 12.30pm-3pm), 6.30pm-9pm Thur-Mon. Open Easter, bank holiday weekends, and from 21 Jun-1 Sep
- **PRICE:** Lunch €19, Dinner €45
- **CREDIT CARDS:** Visa, Mastercard, Laser

NOTES:

Wheelchair access. Food to go. Shop selling produce and cookery books. Cookery classes. See web for details.

DIRECTIONS:

On the Ahakista road just outside the village of Durrus.

LES GOURMANDISES

Patrick & Soizic Kiely
17 Cook Street
Cork, County Cork
+353 (0) 21-425 1959
www.lesgourmandises.ie
info@lesgourmandises.ie

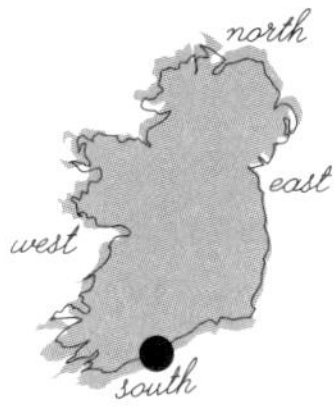

Steady and organic growth and improvement over the years has brought Les Gourmandises to the centre stage in Cork's competitive culinary culture.

Quietly but decisively, Pat and Soizic Kiely have moved to the centre of the culinary stage in Pat's home town. The awards and commendations now come in steadily and consistently, recognising the fusion of superb cooking, great service and excellent style that Les Gourmandises offers.

Their changes over the years have been quiet but decisive. The room was improved from its original simplicity, but not at the expense of comfort. Recently, the innovative market menu has seen a series of plats du jour offered which show the umbilical link between the kitchen and its local suppliers – braised rabbit with choucroute; john dory with creamed celeriac; apple tart with cinnamon ice cream – simple ingredients ennobled by astute and expert cooking. Of course there are starry ingredients that reflect Mr Kiely's time spent learning in starry kitchens – hot and cold foie gras with star anise; terrine of skate and bacon; duck leg with thyme crème brulée – but there is no straining for effect in this restaurant: the food does the talking, and it whispers in your ear.

● **OPEN:** 6pm-9.30pm Mon-Sat
● **PRICE:** Market menu 4-courses, €45, served with glass of wine (served 6pm-10pm Mon-Thur, and 6pm-7pm Fri). A la carte & Tasting menu, €60 Mon-Sat
● **CREDIT CARDS:** Visa, Mastercard, Laser, Amex

● **NOTES:**
Wheelchair access, but no disabled toilet.

● **DIRECTIONS:**
Cook St runs between Patrick St and Oliver Plunkett St.

ISLAND COTTAGE

John Desmond & Ellmary Fenton
Heir Island, Skibbereen
West Cork
+353 (0) 28-38102
www.islandcottage.com

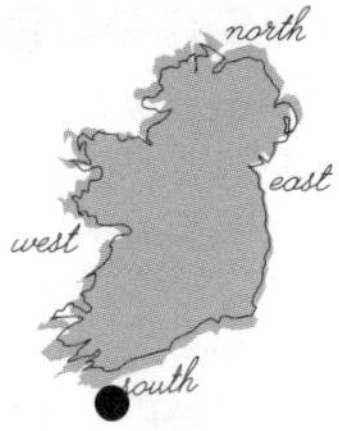

It comes as no surprise to learn that John Desmond is a successful painter. His entire metier has been a painterly, artistic one right from the start.

With a growing number of Irish restaurants nowadays having the nerve to only cook what they are capable of doing at their very best, let us praise one of the chefs who first had the gall to offer a limited template of choice in order to maintain the highest standards. John Desmond created Island Cottage as a one-sitting, no-choice restaurant in order to serve the food he wanted to cook at the level of accomplishment he wanted to achieve. Menus revolve around his signature dishes and his improvisations with them – carpaccio of salmon, or carpaccio of chef-caught mackerel, or marinated salmon on brown bread: roast duck with fennel mayonnaise, or duck legs with onions, or roast duck with rice noodles; then the games with garden fresh salads, and the eternal Gubbeen cheese plate before some stonking puddings: hot chocolate soufflé, or chocolate mousse, or hot lemon soufflé. Like a painter endlessly painting the same scene, and never painting it the same way twice, Mr Desmond has mined his artistic furrow on the canvas of cookery. It has been a privilege to watch.

- **OPEN:** 8pm-midnight, 1 June-15 Sept, Wed-Sat
- **PRICE:** Dinner €45
- **CREDIT CARDS:** No credit cards

NOTES:
Booking essential. No children. No vegetarians or special diets. No deviation from set menu. Max groups of six people high season. Cookery courses from 1 April.

DIRECTIONS:
The shortest ferry trip is from Cunnamore pier, which is signposted to Hare Island off the N71.

10 PLACES FOR

BUSINESS ENTERTAINING

1
AQUA
COUNTY DUBLIN

2
BALZAC
COUNTY DUBLIN

3
BANG CAFÉ
COUNTY DUBLIN

4
CHAPTER ONE
COUNTY DUBLIN

5
L'ECRIVAIN
COUNTY DUBLIN

6
EGG, AVOCA
COUNTY DUBLIN

7
ELY
COUNTY DUBLIN

8
LES GOURMANDISES
COUNTY CORK

9
JAMES STREET SOUTH
NORTHERN IRELAND

10
POULOTS
COUNTY DUBLIN

JACQUES

Jacqueline Barry & Eithne Barry
Phoenix Street, Cork,
County Cork
+353 (0) 21-427 7387
www.jacquesrestaurant.ie
jacquesrestaurant@eircom.net

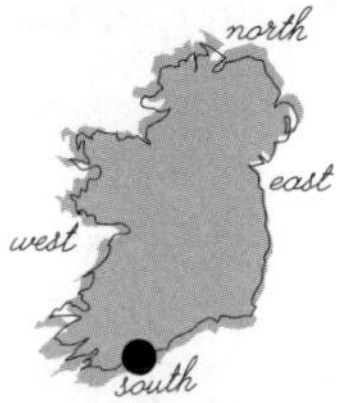

Exhibiting teenybopperish energy and enthusiasm for their calling, despite thirty years at the stove, is how Jacque and Eithne keep Jacques forever young.

Jacque and Eithne are writing daily menus in Jacques nowadays, proving that after 30 years in the business, this pair and their crew are as focused on first principles as ever. On September 11th 2007, they offered food that would give comfort to those for whom that day is an always painful anniversary: mackerel with roast beets and horseradish; Caroline's Piedmontese peppers with buffalo mozzarella; brill with chive hollandaise, courgette and tomato; lamb with hummus and buttered cucumber; Gubbeen pork with apple sauce and deep-fried sage; potato roulade with Bluebell Falls goat's cheese. Knowing how to hit those comfort zones is the key to the girls' 30 years of success. But knowing how to stay youthful, and how to stay inspired by the business of cooking and serving food, is just as important. Like the best south-west female masters – Kay and Marog; Myrtle and Darina, Maura Foley of Kenmare – Jacque and Eithne seem to have discovered the elixir of eternal life, because 30 years in the restaurant trade is an eternity. They understand that comfort ensures sustainability.

- **OPEN:** 6pm-10pm Mon-Sat
- **PRICE:** Dinner €42
- **CREDIT CARDS:** Visa, Mastercard, Laser, Amex

NOTES:

Early bird dinner, 2 courses, 6pm-7pm Mon-Sat, €21.90
Outside catering for small or large parties available.
See website.

DIRECTIONS:

Just behind the main post office in the centre of the city.

LONGUEVILLE HOUSE

William & Aisling O'Callaghan
The President's Restaurant
Mallow, North Cork
+353 (0) 22-47156
www.longuevillehouse.ie
info@longuevillehouse.ie

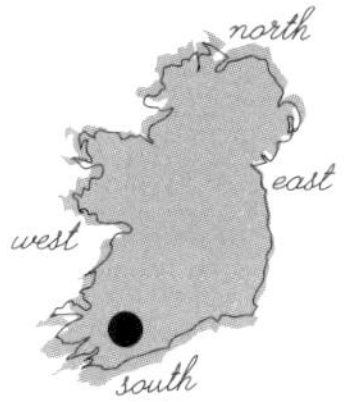

Cooking of sublime grace and harmony, with unique flavours and pedigree, is the Longueville House USP.

You will find William and Aisling O'Callaghan working hard at the Mahon Point Farmers' Market on Thursday morning every week, as this talented couple extend their reach beyond Longueville House into their expanding retailing of Longueville products. Their products are superlative, and utterly distinct, the work of people who are as wedded to the garden as they are to the challenges of the kitchen.

On a recent visit, Eamon Barrett pronounced the cooking to be "among the best Longueville dinners I've ever eaten - and that is saying something." For ourselves, the latest dinner started with roast Dublin Bay prawns with bisque, then risotto of wild girolles with Imokilly cheddar, then freshly caught Blackwater salmon with herb crust, then Newmarket beef fillet with horseradish mayonnaise, and an autumn tarte tatin with ice cream made with Longueville's own apple brandy. The progression of foods was symphonic, textured, measured, expert. The calm of the house and dining room makes it perfect for a quiet getaway, but we like it much better with a crowd.

- **OPEN:** 6.30pm-8.30pm Mon-Sun
- **PRICE:** Dinner €60-€85
- **CREDIT CARDS:** Visa, Mastercard, Laser, Amex

NOTES:

Limited wheelchair access. Recommended for vegetarians. Snack bar lunch 12.30pm-5pm

DIRECTIONS:

5km from Mallow when travelling in direction of Killarney, and well signposted from the road.

O'CALLAGHAN-WALSHE

Sean Kearney
The Square, Rosscarbery
West Cork
+353 (0) 23-48125
funfish@indigo.ie

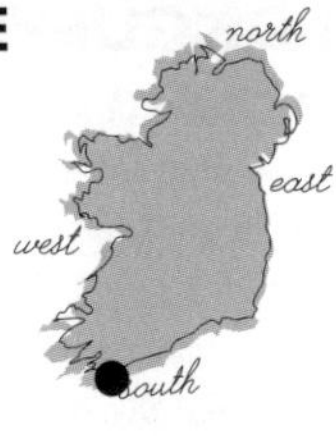

Sean's wit is as red-hot as Martina's cooking in O'C-W; as potent a West Cork combination as you can find.

"We also try, as far as possible, not to follow trends or fashions. God knows it's hard enough for us to sear a scallop or grill a bit of squid and do it right, as often as possible, without infusing or cappuccinoing or serenading the buggers to death." He is the wittiest patron, without a doubt, is Sean Kearney, but his wisdom is as great as his wit. Last time in O'C-W, we had perfect grilled squid – particularly perfect, actually – and perfect seared scallops – particularly perfect, actually. We also had perfect Dover sole, and Roxanne's unique Big Prawn scampi was consumed in the blink of an eye, as was the john dory and the fine spicy fish cakes and the superb turbot with lemon butter. Nothing fussy, just simple perfection from a kitchen that knows what it wants to do and that knows how to do it, with sublime service from a man who surely holds the patent on West Cork sangfroid. There is nowhere quite like this wild, brilliant, unorthodox restaurant, simply because it has no truck with fashion or the latest trends, and so exists in its own time and place: sui generis.

- **OPEN:** 6.30pm-9.30pm Tue-Sun. Weekends only Oct-May
- **PRICE:** Dinner €50
- **CREDIT CARDS:** Visa, Mastercard, Laser

NOTES:
Wheelchair access, but no disabled toilet. Reservations recommended. Vegetarians please pre-book.

DIRECTIONS:
On the main square in Rosscarbery. In the centre of the village, turn off at the Celtic Ross hotel.

OVER THE MOON

Jennifer & François Conradie
46 Bridge Street
Skibbereen
West Cork
+353 (0) 28-22100
www.overthemoonskibbereen.com

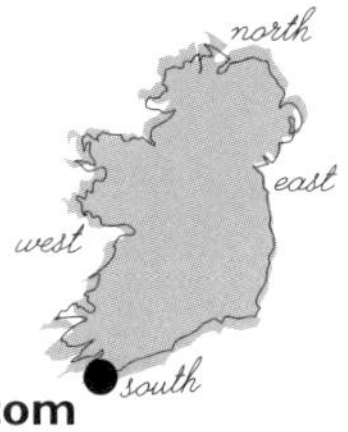

A bright new light with bright cooking, Jennifer and Francois's OTM is aiming for the stars.

It took no time at all after Jennifer and François had opened up in Over The Moon, having spent a couple of years working in Cork city after spells in the UK and South Africa, for the West Cork gossip to be spreading far and wide about what they were doing.
"Definitely 100 Best material," says a local chef. "Excellent...The lunch and dinner menus are sensibly restricted to a few well-prepared dishes, the wines are excellent," says a friend. Both are right. This is a smart operation, and a great addition to the idiosyncratic West Cork food culture. The concision of the menus, and the careful attention to detail in sourcing, means that the dishes are tip-top: salmon gravadlax with horseradish, warm potato and beetroot; crab mayonnaise with sourdough bread and crisp fennel. François likes to contrast flavour and texture elements – chicken salad with soya beans and roasted peppers; scallops with Gubbeen bacon; whipped cream with a pistachio chocolate brownie – and it makes for eating that is light, flavourful and direct. A short list of wines, excellent service, OTM.

- **OPEN:** noon-3pm, 6pm-10pm Mon-Sat, 12.30pm-8pm Sun
- **PRICE:** Lunch €20, Dinner €38
- **CREDIT CARDS:** Visa, Mastercard, Laser

NOTES:
No wheelchair access.

DIRECTIONS:
Upstairs across from Eldon's Hotel, at the west end of Skibbereen.

TODDIE'S @THE KINSALE BREWERY

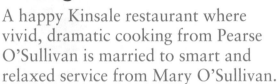

Pearse & Mary O'Sullivan
The Glen, Kinsale, West Cork
+353 (0) 21-477 7769
www.toddies.ie
toddies@eircom.net

A happy Kinsale restaurant where vivid, dramatic cooking from Pearse O'Sullivan is married to smart and relaxed service from Mary O'Sullivan.

Grated fresh horseradish with an avocado and prawn salad. Jamaican jerk chicken with a modish Caesar salad. Wholemeal pizza base with Ardsallagh cheese, artichoke and rocket. Crab cake with Asian pesto. Hake with a fennel purée and coriander buttered clams. Fillet steak with Perigordine sauce. Chocolate and orange crème brulée. Pearse O'Sullivan never does quite what you expect him to do.

His cooking has curious, intriguing grace notes, unexpected shifts of emphasis. He works to a different beat compared to the mainstream cooking of his peers. It makes eating in the handsome and happy space of Toddie's a challenge, as well as a delight, as this talented chef takes diversions and detours around many dishes. Of course, he is cooking in a popular tourist town, so there are staples such as sole on the bone; terrine of foie gras; scampi with tartare sauce; breast of duck with caramelised apples and Calvados, all delivered with sharpness and effortless competence. But we like it when he mixes it up a bit, when the drama of the dinner really unfolds.

- **OPEN:** 6.30pm-10.30pm Mon-Sat high season, closed Mon low season. Closed Jan & Feb
- **PRICE:** Dinner €45
- **CREDIT CARDS:** Visa, Mastercard, Laser, Amex

NOTES:
Wheelchair access.

DIRECTIONS:
From the centre of Kinsale, looking up towards the White House restaurant, turn right. Toddie's is two doors along, upstairs, through the brewery gates.

AN BONNAN BUI

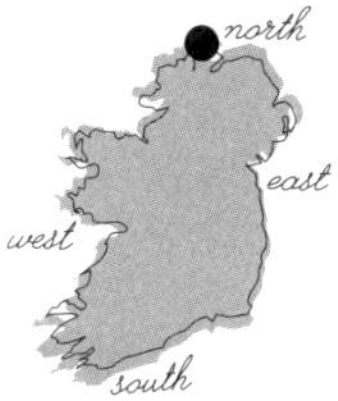

Martin & Monica Kelly
Pier Road, Rathmullan
County Donegal
+353 (0) 74-915 8453
www.anbonnanbui.com
bonnanbui@yahoo.ie

ABB offers superbly executed global cooking, with wildly invigorating tastes and lush, rich textures.

The superlatives seem to be on the tip of everyone's tongue when it comes to Martin and Monica's An Bonnan Bui.
"One of the best meals we had all holiday... one of the best chocolate cakes I've ever had... excellent service... great atmosphere."
"The most amazing atmosphere and the food, menu and wine list are exquisite." And that is the reaction of just a couple of happy readers who found the trip to the farthermost northernmost reaches of Donegal to be well worth their time, thanks to the great inventiveness and originality of this talented couple. Monica's Brazilian background gives a lively and surprising lift to her cooking, offering dishes that are both pungent and punchy, but it is the confidence shown through the menu's range of dishes, from Portuguese fish balls, to kibbeh with pine nuts and mint, to Brazilian seafood moqueca, that is ABB's winning formula. There is a thoughtful children's menu, and prices for both food and the excellent wines are super-keen. A long way to go for dinner, and worth it.

- **OPEN:** Mon-Sun 5.30pm-9.30pm. Limited hours off season, ring to check
- **PRICE:** Dinner €35
- **CREDIT CARDS:** Visa, Mastercard, Laser

NOTES:
Full wheelchair access once you've negotiated the steps into the restaurant.

DIRECTIONS:
Head down main street to the shore, but instead of driving down to the beach turn left onto Pier road.

AROMA

Tom Dooley & Arturo de Alba
Donegal Craft Village
Donegal
County Donegal
+353 (0) 74-972 3222
tomandarturo@yahoo.com

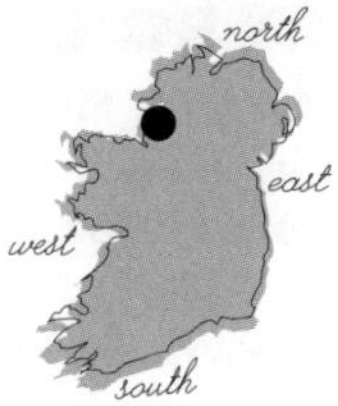

There's a peaceful, easy feelin' about Tom and Arturo's iconic Aroma, the most super cooking and super baking in the most simple place imaginable.

Tom and Arturo have a lovely, easy, gently paced way of doing things in Aroma. They never seem to rush. They let the food come together in its own time, whether it is Tom's superb baking or Arturo's superb cooking for the day's dishes. When the food is ready, then one of the girls will patiently, carefully, write the titles of the day's dishes on the blackboard over the kitchen hatch: toasted ciabatta with mince and raisins; prawn and avocado salad with chive oil; creamy chicken, mushroom and garlic casserole; Aroma club with roast beef, tomato, roasted peppers, brie and mustard mayo.

The food reads simple, but the flavours are so layered, composed and polished that the food has all the magic of the sublime. These guys understand the elegance of simplicity, and the magic of commonplace things: good brown bread; good sweet cakes, a perfect risotto, lovely stuffed peppers, excellent espresso. What is the secret of Aroma? Could be its rhythm, maybe? The food has its rhythm. The room has its rhythm. The rhythm of life? Well, it's certainly the Rhythm of Eating, nothing less.

- **OPEN:** 9.30am-5.30pm Mon-Sat
- **PRICE:** Lunch €18.50
- **CREDIT CARDS:** Visa, Mastercard, Laser

NOTES:

Wheelchair access, but no disabled toilet.

DIRECTIONS:

Take the old road directly into Donegal town, avoiding the new bypass. The Craft Village is a collection of single-storey craft workshops south of the town and clearly signposted, 2km or so outside the town.

THE MILL RESTAURANT

Derek & Susan Alcorn
Figart, Dunfanaghy
North Donegal
+353 (0) 74-913 6985
www.themillrestaurant.com
themillrestaurant@oceanfree.net

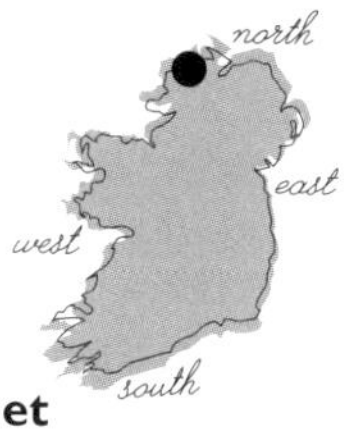

Great to eat, and great to think about after you have eaten it, Derek Alcorn's cooking is exceptional.

Derek Alcorn is one of those chefs with the gift for making their food utterly memorable. Right from the first time we ate his cooking, seven years ago now, the dishes seemed created not simply to be delicious, but to be unforgettable. Good to eat, and just as good to think. Salmon and crab terrine with crème fraiche and pesto. Brill with basil mash, or that same mash served with superb Horn Head mackerel. The fillet steak with grated spuds and pancetta. The caramelised rice pudding. The chicken livers and black pudding with rosemary porridge fritter. The seared scallops with crispy anchovies. The rhubarb crumble tart.
Most memorably, of course, was the dessert which seared itself onto the memories of the young McKenna children a few years back: Mr Ice Cream Man. So, it doesn't even matter if you aren't much more than a toddler: Mr Alcorn will leave you with an unforgettable food memory. And everything else about The Mill is just as sweet to recall: the great service under Susan Alcorn, the comfort and calm, the amazing value for money. Ace.

- **OPEN:** 7pm-9pm Tue-Sun (closed Halloween-Easter. Weekends only off season)
- **PRICE:** Dinner €45
- **CREDIT CARDS:** Visa, Mastercard, Laser, Amex

NOTES:

Wheelchair access to restaurant. Recommmended for children. Six guestrooms.

DIRECTIONS:

From Letterkenny take the N56 through Dunfanaghy. The Mill is 1km past the village on right.

ALEXIS BAR & GRILL

Alan & Patrick O'Reilly
17/18 Patrick Street
Dun Laoghaire, County Dublin
+353 (0) 1-280 8872
www.alexis.ie
bookings@alexis.ie

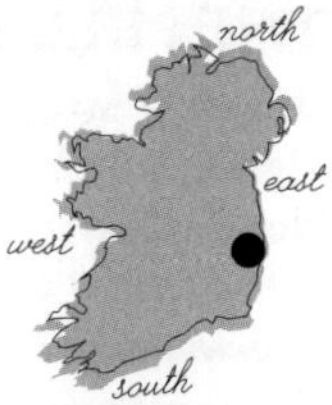

Leslie Williams hadn't finished his starter in Alexis before saying, "I'll be back!" Liked it, then.

Not only did Leslie decide that he would be back after only several bites, he also decided that: the "home-made chips, which were thin, crispy and perfectly seasoned and, at a mere €3, deserve to be ordered with every course, including dessert". Chips with dessert. Even Ferran Adria wouldn't have thought of that.
So, what else was good? The mash was declared "as good as it gets". Braised shoulder of lamb Niçoise was "melt in the mouth tender, and the combination of braising flavours were complementary, without in any way overwhelming the delicate flavours of the lamb". Harry Buckley's grilled rib-eye steak was thick and rare, and served with perfect potato gratin. In the interests of research, Mr Williams ordered three puds – with three portions of fries, one imagines – and chocolate brownie with vanilla ice cream, peach Melba, and fresh fruit tart with crème anglaise were right on the money.
The only downside was some curtness from the staff, but otherwise Alan and Patrick O'Reilly's restaurant is one of the brightest new stars of the Dublin southside.

● **OPEN:** 12.30pm-2.30pm, 5.30pm-10pm Tue-Fri, 5.30pm-10pm Sat, 12.30pm-3pm, 5.30pm-9pm Sun
● **PRICE:** Lunch €14-€18, Dinner €30-€35
● **CREDIT CARDS:** Visa, Mastercard, Laser, Amex

● **NOTES:**
Wheelchair access.

● **DIRECTIONS:**
Patricks Street runs up the hill, almost opposite Marine Road. Driving through Dun Laoghaire you have to pass through Patrick St because of the one-way system.

AQUA

Richard Clery & Charlie Smith
1 West Pier
Howth, County Dublin
+353 (0) 1-832 0690
www.aqua.ie
dine@aqua.ie

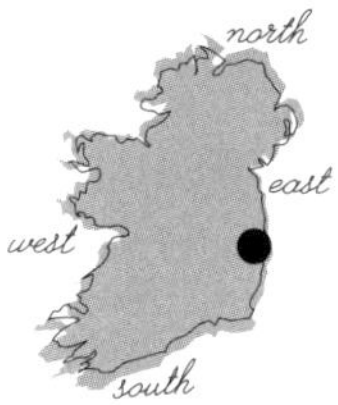

The north county Dublin solid sender never disappoints, and the comfort and lushness of the experience is something you can never tire of.

Amazing views over the sea from a location at the end of the pier. Lovely art works. Cosy, comfortable rooms. Sublime food. Svelte service. Aqua is a place which is masterly in the arts of making you feel special, whether it's the early bird for two on a Tuesday evening, or your latest thirtysomething birthday with a bunch of friends on Friday night, kicking off with the bubbly.
That striving for comfort touches everything they do. No one is rewriting Escoffier in here or challenging Ferran Adria. Instead their modus operandi is consistent excellence, and bourgeois comfort, and they achieve both with gas in the tank, and without any po-faced solemnity. This means you can have fish and chips, or lobster with foie gras if it is really your birthday, or you can play safe with their greatest hits such as sole on the bone, cod with basil bearnaise, or beef fillet with wild mushrooms and baby onions. This is serious, professional cooking in a serious, professional restaurant, and the consistent excellence and dedication to the culinary arts shown by the crew over the years is most gratifying, and pleasing.

- **OPEN:** 12.30pm-3pm Tue-Sat, 5.30pm-midnight Mon-Sat, 12pm-4pm, 6.30pm-9.30pm Sun & Bank hol evenings.
- **PRICE:** Lunch €29.95, Dinner €40-€50
- **CREDIT CARDS:** Visa, Mastercard, Laser

NOTES:
Early bird 5.30pm-7pm Mon-Fri, 5.30pm-6.30pm Sat, €29.95. Wheelchair access (stair lift)

DIRECTIONS:
At the end of Howth West Pier, five mins from DART.

BALZAC

Paul Flynn
35 Dawson Street, Dublin 2
County Dublin
+353 (0) 1-677 8611
www.balzac.ie
info@balzac.ie

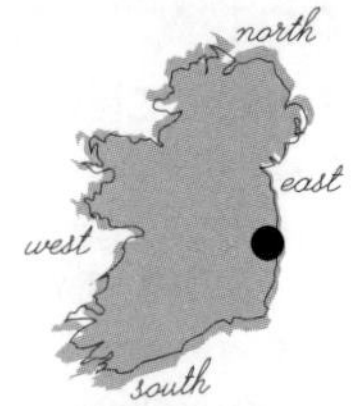

A brilliant resurrection has seen Balzac emerge as one of the hot new Dublin addresses.

The old La Stampa had slipped off every food lover's radar, but Paul Flynn, of Dungarvan's The Tannery, has proven himself the master of the phoenix in resurrecting this beautiful room, renaming it Balzac, and gracing it with the classic cooking it needs.

The menu melds Flynn classics – crab crème brulée; crubeens and colcannon; onion and cider soup – with brasserie staples – oysters mignonette; rib eye with bernaise mousseline (served with perfect fries); slow-cooked beef with horseradish and parsley crust; brandade of cod; duck fat roast potatoes; chocolate truffle cake – and the fit has proven perfect, with Jay Collier in the kitchen showing the discipline needed to make such a big room work smoothly, and bringing elegance and rusticity to the food in equal measure. Flynn and his team have taken their time to make sure things have worked out right, and have been rewarded with a restaurant that is once again back on the food lover's radar. And, mercy be, the Knuttel paintings are all gone, so art lovers as well as food lovers can enjoy this glam room.

- **OPEN:** 12.30pm-2.30pm Mon-Fri, 6pm-11pm Mon-Sat, 5pm-10pm Sun
- **PRICE:** Lunch €22.50-€28, Dinner €35-€50
- **CREDIT CARDS:** Visa, Mastercard, Laser, Amex

NOTES:

No wheelchair access, though they are happy to help customers with disabilities.

DIRECTIONS:

Opposite the Mansion House, near the St Stephen's Green end of Dawson Street.

BANG CAFÉ

Lorcan Gribbin
11 Merrion Row
Dublin 2, County Dublin
+353 (0) 1-676 0898
www.bangrestaurant.com

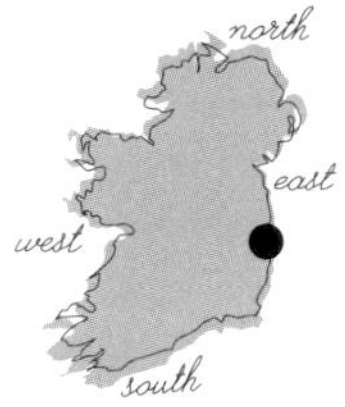

One of the slickest and most assured of the metropolitan dining elite, Bang is brassy, busy and fun, with fine, precise cooking from chef Lorcan Gribbin.

The presence of Gold River Farm, an outstanding and pioneering organic farm in County Wicklow run by the Pearce and Winterbottom families, on the list of specialist suppliers to Bang shows just where Lorcan Gribbin's heart lies. This is a serious chef, who insists on the most exceptional of produce, and the quality of produce is matched by the quality of execution in Mr Gribbin's cooking. Bang is a restaurant that has been on top of its game for several years now, and the completeness of the experience is helped by wise and knowledgeable service that puts the icing on the cake of a really fine metropolitan dining experience.Starters. Grills. Pastas & Salads. Main Courses. Side Orders. Desserts. What to choose from his lightly unconventional menu arrangement for dinner. Double-rib lamb cutlets with garlic confit; oven-roasted sea trout with braised Savoy cabbage; perhaps one of their signature salads such as confit chicken with bacon and frisée, and of course those who admire the kitchen's sense of humour will no doubt plump for the BANGers & Mash. Lovely cooking, grown-up place.

- **OPEN:** 12.30pm-3pm Mon-Sat; 6pm-10.30pm Mon-Wed; 6pm-11pm Thu-Sat. Closed Sun
- **PRICE:** Lunch €30, Dinner €45
- **CREDIT CARDS:** Visa, Mastercard, Laser

NOTES:
No wheelchair access.

DIRECTIONS:
The restaurant is just beyond St Stephen's Green, beside the Bank of Ireland cash machine, where the road narrows.

BON APPETIT

Oliver Dunne
9 St James Terrace
Malahide, County Dublin
+353 (0) 1-845 0314
www.bonappetit.ie
info@bonappetit.ie

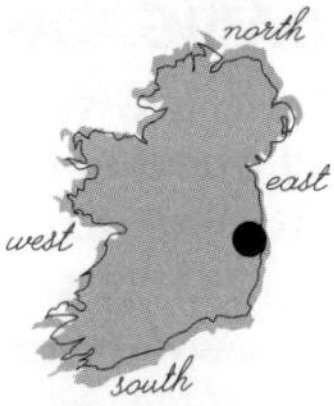

"I can honestly say it's one of the most impressive restaurants I've been to in this country."

Caroline Byrne's summary of a dinner in Oliver Dunne's swish restaurant, as quoted above, then went on to say that there was "almost nothing you could criticize. Also, at 65euro for three courses it's great value". So, stellar cooking from Oliver Dunne and his team, but then that was always to be expected from this chef. He knows his ingredients, so there are lots of – for instance – autumnal elements for a harvest-time dinner – game, roasted nuts, woodland mushrooms – and the ingredients are skilfully integrated into dishes that soon have you purring with pleasure: boudin of skate and braised pork belly with girolle purée and crispy capers; roast breast of quail and confit legs with red onion purée; confit rabbit with beetroot purée and roast artichoke dressed with a balsamic reduction; Dover sole in a red wine sauce with fondant potato. This is rich cooking, but the balance and integrity of the elements, the alliance between classical techniques and modern innovations – Szechwan pepper foam on top of white chocolate crème anglaise, for instance – is spot on, and BA has already taken off.

- **OPEN:** 7pm-9.30pm Tue-Sat, 12.30pm-2.30pm Fri
- **PRICE:** Dinner €65, Lunch €35-€65
- **CREDIT CARDS:** Visa, Mastercard, Laser, Amex

NOTES:
No wheelchair access.

DIRECTIONS:
The restaurant is located in the centre of the Georgian Terrace in front of the estuary.

CAVISTON'S

Peter Caviston
59 Glasthule Road, Sandycove
Dun Laoghaire, County Dublin
+353 (0) 1-280 9245
www.cavistons.com
info@cavistons.com

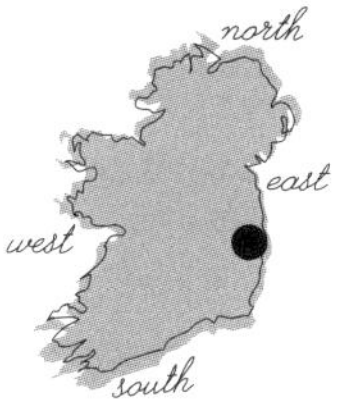

Noel Cusack and his team are as dedicated and disciplined today after a decade of cooking the freshest fish.

It has become a fashionable commonplace for fish restaurants to also have a wet fish counter these days, but what is something of an affectation elsewhere is actually the seabed of the Caviston's operation. This brilliant seafood restaurant grew out of the celebrated fish shop that adjoins the restaurant, and selling wet fish begat the cooking of wet fish.

So, whilst Peter Caviston and his crew are flogging it in the shop, Noel Cusack and his crew are frying it in the restaurant, and both do what they have to do superbly. Mr Cusack waits until he has the day's catch in hand, then composes the daily menu at the speed of light, and then for the three daily servings of lunch it is all magnificent mayhem as the good people of South Dublin are fed on baked oyster with coriander and pinenuts; Boston shrimps with lemon and herb dressing; King scallops with saffron and basil sauce; monkfish with Dijon potatoes and curry oil; the splendid seafood pie; grilled mackerel on the bone. Some folk are so fixated on the fish they foolishly overlook some very good puddings.

- **OPEN:** three lunch sittings per day: noon, 1.30pm, 3pm Tue-Fri; noon, 1.45pm, 3.15pm Sat
- **PRICE:** Lunch €45
- **CREDIT CARDS:** Visa, Mastercard, Laser, Amex

NOTES:
Reservations essential. Wheelchair access but no disabled toilet

DIRECTIONS:
In the centre of Sandycove village, beside Caviston's Deli.

CHAPTER ONE

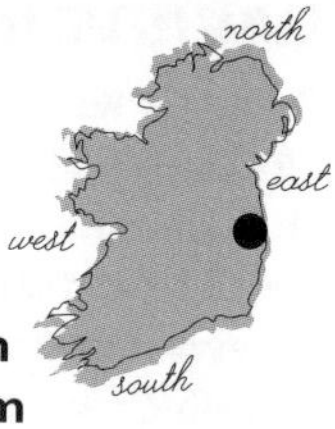

Ross Lewis & Martin Corbett
18-19 Parnell Square
Dublin 1
+353 (0) 1-873 2266
www.chapteronerestaurant.com
info@chapteronerestaurant.com

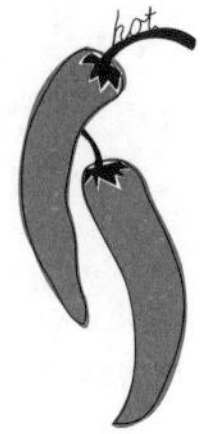

Ross Lewis and Martin Corbett have created not just a restaurant icon, but a veritable cultural icon, in Chapter One.

Here is what Ross Lewis and his crew cooked as a dinner to celebrate the produce of some well-known Irish artisans. For Jane Murphy: salad of Ardsallagh goat's cheese and beetroot. Michael Healy: pheasant and chestnut soup. Ed Hick: cured venison and foie gras salad, pig's trotter boudin, watercress, apple and raisin, hazelnut dressing. Sally Barnes: smoked haddock and leek gratin. Maurice Kettyle: spiced daube of beef, onion purée and ceps. Jane and Louis Grubb: Crozier Blue cheese, white truffle honey. And a comice pear, cappuccino mousse and brioche, to conclude.
The meal was technically flawless, and inspirational in terms of flavours, textures and execution. But, of course, its real significance – its genius – lies in the fact that the Chapter One crew draw their own inspiration from the artisans who produce food for them, and this symbiotic dependency is the secret of the success of this extraordinary restaurant. Chapter One isn't just part of the food culture: it is part of the artistic and agricultural culture of the country, transcending food, making art.

- **OPEN:** 12.30pm-2pm Tue-Fri; 6pm-10pm Tue-Sat
- **PRICE:** Lunch €35, Dinner €60-€70
- **CREDIT CARDS:** Visa, Mastercard, Laser, Amex

- **NOTES:**

Limited wheelchair access - basement restaurant.
Pre-theatre, 6pm-7.40pm, €35 (starter, main course, then come back for dessert).

- **DIRECTIONS:**

In the basement of the Dublin Writers' Museum.

L'ECRIVAIN

Derry & Sallyanne Clarke
109 Lower Baggot Street
Dublin 2
+353 (0) 1-661 1919
www.lecrivain.com
enquiries@lecrivain.com

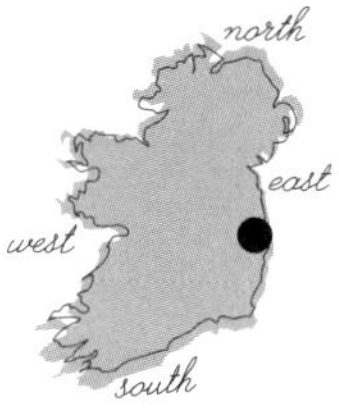

Dream-like in its culinary and restauranty business, L'Ecrivain is a magic carpet ride of sheer brilliance from a brilliant team.

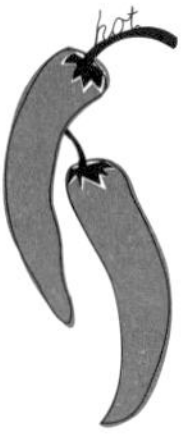

"Perhaps it is part of the magic of L'Ecrivain that it subjects each one of its clients to the same grand illusion." The writer Hugh Leonard wrote those words in his introduction – his celebratory introduction – to Derry and Sallyanne Clarke's book on their restaurant, *More than a Cookbook*. Mr Leonard is quite right. Entering into the experience of L'Ecrivain is like an illusion because it can seem all too perfect, all too elemental, all too magical. The vividness of the staff and their brilliant characters. The glam of the room, and its thrilling clientele, the most vivid snapshot of Dublin at play. And then the ambrosial cooking, a modern Irish style of food that reads sensible – rack of lamb with spiced root vegetables, pomme fondant, lemon and thyme jus; veal liver with whipped cheese and onion potatoes, crisp bacon, onion gravy; steamed Irish salmon with pea and garlic purée, saffron and roasted red peppers – but which, on the plate, is as vivacious and radical as any sport of nature. The illusion, of course, is founded on solid hard work, but it's a hypnotic, intense pleasure.

- **OPEN:** 12.30pm-2pm Mon-Fri; 7pm-10.30pm Mon-Sat
- **PRICE:** Lunch €40-€50, Dinner €85
- **CREDIT CARDS:** Visa, Mastercard, Laser, Amex

NOTES:
Limited wheelchair access on ground floor. Service charge on food and wine only (10%)

DIRECTIONS:
Through a small archway, just beside Lad Lane, across the road from Bank of Ireland HQ on Baggot Street.

10 PLACES

TO DRESS UP FOR

1

BALLYMALOE HOUSE
COUNTY CORK

2

THE BALLYMORE INN
COUNTY KILDARE

3

BALZAC
COUNTY DUBLIN

4

BIALANN & SEOMRAÍ SO INIS MEÁIN
ARAN ISLANDS

5

CAYENNE
NORTHERN IRELAND

6

L'ECRIVAIN
COUNTY DUBLIN

7

FALLON & BYRNE
COUNTY DUBLIN

8

FISHY FISHY CAFÉ
COUNTY CORK

9

LOCKS
COUNTY DUBLIN

10

TOWN BAR & GRILL
COUNTY DUBLIN

EDEN

Jay Bourke
Meeting House Square
Temple Bar, Dublin 2
+353 (0) 1-670 5372
www.edenrestaurant.ie
eden@edenrestaurant.ie

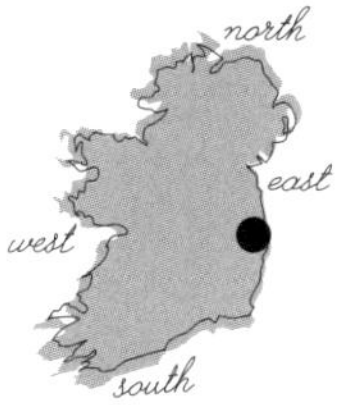

With a second Eden open at Jay Bourke's country pile, Bellinter, the original formula is proving its adaptability, durability and excellence.

There are two Edens in operation nowadays, as the restaurant in Jay Bourke's swish Bellinter House in County Meath – see the entry in the sister volume to this book, the *Bridgestone 100 Best Places to Stay 2008* – also bears the title of the great Temple Bar stalwart. But even with a kid brother in the family, it is still hard to outshine the mix of savvy food, style and service which is what Eden Temple Bar has offered for over a decade.
Founding chef Eleanor Walsh has moved on to new challenges, but head chef Michael Durkan maintains the roll-call of great dishes that one simply can't tire of eating – the signature smokies with their creamy, cheesy flavours; the punch and succulence of scallops with smoked paprika aioli; the comfort of organic beef and Guinness stew; the toothy savour of wild mallard with game pie sauce; the melting meld of lamb shank with mash.
This is sure-fire cooking in a restaurant that maintains enviable standards, and which, however many newcomers may arrive on the scene, still holds its own as a glamorous destintion for a big date, or for weekend brunch.

- **OPEN:** 12.30pm-3pm Mon-Fri; noon-3pm Sat & Sun; 6pm-10.30pm Mon-Sun
- **PRICE:** Lunch €22-€24, Dinner from €42
- **CREDIT CARDS:** Visa, Mastercard, Laser, Amex

NOTES:
Wheelchair access on ground floor, but no disabled toilet. Pre-theatre menu, 6pm-7pm Sun-Thur, €27

DIRECTIONS:
Meeting House Square is between Eustace Street and Dame Street in the heart of Temple Bar.

ELY

Erik Robson & Michelle Moyles
●Ely Wine Bar, 22 Ely Place, D2 +353 (0) 1-676 8986 ●Ely CHQ, IFSC, D1 & 672 0010 ●Ely HQ, Hanover Quay, D2 & 633 9986
www.elywinebar.ie

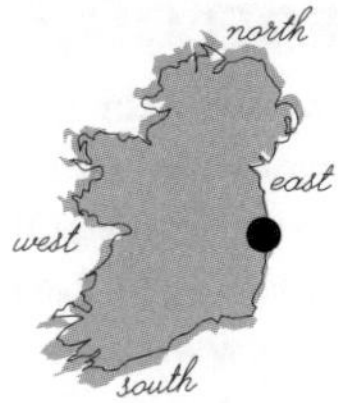

The mighty trio of Ely, Ely CHQ and Ely HQ. Which to choose? Absolutely the most delicious Dublin dining dilemma.

Ely presents a dilemma: Which one should you choose? Well, last time, we chose Ely HQ in the brand new Hanover Quay. The place was kickin'. The punters were groovy – bankers, rock bands drinking Bolly, hip young women – and were almost as groovy as the staff. And we ate so well it just wasn't true, with chef Tom Doyle firing out some inspired cooking – pitch-perfect pavé of lamb sweetbreads with crushed hazelnuts and Wexford honey; roast brie in smoked bacon; awesome bangers and mash for the kids; roast veal with celeriac purée and black pudding samosas; excellent vegetarian crepe with ratatouille. Ace food, ace place. But, then... so are all three Elys, from the little original on Ely Place to the swish Ely CHQ just north of the river. Erik and Michelle Robson's achievement seems to us to be amongst the most considerable in Dublin hospitality in recent years, and their secret is to understand polite service, good food and great wines, and to inspire their crews to match them every step of the way. Which one to choose? No dilemma was ever so delicious.

● **OPEN:** CHQ: Lunch & Dinner Mon-Sun; HQ lunch Mon-Fri, Dinner Mon-Sun; Ely noon-late Mon-Sun
● **PRICE:** Lunch €22, Dinner €35
● **CREDIT CARDS:** Visa, Mastercard, Laser Amex

● **NOTES:**
Wheelchair access in both CHQ and HQ. Also baby changing facilities.

● **DIRECTIONS:**
Ely Place runs off Merrion Row. CHQ is north of the River Liffey, beside IFSC. HQ overlooks Hanover Quay.

FALLON & BYRNE

Fiona McHugh, Paul Byrne & Brian Fallon
Exchequer Building
11-17 Exchequer Street, Dublin 2
+353 (0) 1-472 1010
www.fallonandbyrne.com
feedback@fallonandbyrne.com

F&B is proof that Dublin has joined the great European capitals in offering dynamic restaurant entertainment and fun.

Barcelona? Excuse me? Excuse me? Who needs Barcelona, when you can have Fallon & Byrne on a Dublin Saturday night, the room heaving and kicking, pumping with energy, brio and style, the gloriously executed cooking of Tom Meenahan and his team lifting everyone's spirits higher and higher and higher. Anyone who can remember Dublin in the dour 'oul times of the 1970's and 1980's, and who walks into this great space on a Saturday night in the 21st century, can only feel that they have entered the Dublin of their dreams, a city with the power of New York, the style of Madrid, the culture of Rome, the energy of Barcelona. Is this real? Pinch me! Anyhow, that was how John McKenna felt on a Saturday night in F&B, but Mrs McKenna and the McKenna children were too busy scoffing delicious food, perched on stools at the bar, to reflect on what it is that Fallon & Byrne has achieved. So, forget the past and just luxuriate in the present, with perfect sirloin with bearnaise, milk-poached belly of pork with cloved red cabbage, great grilled chicken and chips for the youngsters. Amazing.

- **OPEN:** 12.30pm-3pm Mon-Sat, 12.30pm-4pm Sun, 6pm-10pm Mon-Thu, 6pm-11pm Fri & Sat, 6pm-9pm Sun
- **PRICE:** Lunch €35, Dinner €45
- **CREDIT CARDS:** Visa, Mastercard, Laser, Amex

NOTES:

Full wheelchair access.

DIRECTIONS:

Exchequer St leads off Wicklow St, which itself leads off Dublin's main shopping street, Grafton St.

GREEN ISLAND

20 Moore Street
Dublin 1

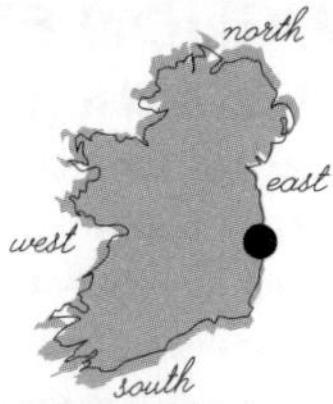

"In terms of taste, variety, authenticity, atmosphere and value, the best Chinese I've ever eaten in."

That was the opinion of Caroline Byrne of the Bridgestone canton, after dinner in TGI. Signalled by two bright red Chinese lanterns hanging from the canopy, the Green Island offers the wildest queer gear: delicious drunk duck; fried pig's intestines with Chinese sauerkraut; spicy, fried, dried jelly fish; "special taste" pork hocks. This is wild Southern Chinese food, though don't worry that it is all as strange as this: there are more standard dishes such as sweet and sour and a decent array of vegetarian choices also.
The staff smile sweetly, and do their best to cross the language barrier – bringing a Mandarin speaker isn't essential, but it sure would help – but language is soon left adrift in a cacophony of munching, slurping, relishing, enjoying and quaffing. There are no starters/mains/afters as such, so just pile in with meat dumplings, fried kai lan, fried pork belly with Chinese cabbage and star anise, crispy roast squid, fried sliced duck, some good fried rice, lots of beer, and marvel at the tiny size of the bill.

- **OPEN:** 11am-11pm Mon-Sun
- **PRICE:** Lunch €12, Dinner €25
- **CREDIT CARDS:** No Credit Cards

- **NOTES:**

No wheelchair access.

- **DIRECTIONS:**

Turn left at the top of O'Connell Street onto Parnell Street, take the second left onto Moore Street and it's on the left-hand side, with two distinct lanterns hung outside.

L'GUEULETON

Declan O'Regan
1 Fade Street
Dublin 2
+353 (0) 1-675 3708
www.lgueuleton.com
info@lgueuleton.com

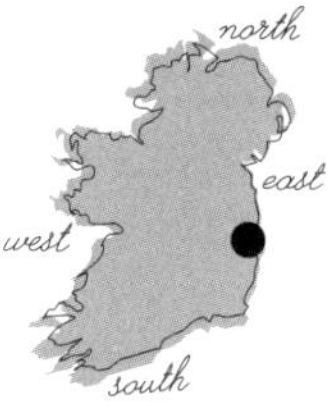

Guys! Did you know that many young women meet their girlfriends for an early dinner in L'Gueuleton! But first, practice pronouncing that darn name.

Declan O'Regan's funky bistro rocks as steady as ever, keeping things simple, charming, smart. It's no surprise to see that so many young single women should choose to meet their friends here, sharing a couple of starters, then maybe a main course between two before a belt of coffees, with a glass of wine each. Smart city folk whose wallets are too tight to mention thrive on the loose and informal style of L'Gueuleton. They know how to use it to get what they want, and the restaurant responds in kind, with requests to divvy up main courses met with a calm, "Of course", whether it's two twentysomething girls or a McKenna parent asking if the boys could share a dish of Toulouse sausages with Lyonnaise potatoes. The cooking fuses a Sugar Club/Skye Gyngell style of food, with roasty flavours offset by grace notes, such as pleasingly bitter leaves, pungent capers, good Savoy cabbage. They know how to roast a belly of pork nice and slowly, they know how to grill a chicken and – shocking, we know – but their duck egg mayonnaise is really very, very good. Service is great, value is only excellent.

- **OPEN:** 12.30pm-3pm, 6pm-10pm Mon-Sat
- **PRICE:** Lunch €29, Dinner €40
- **CREDIT CARDS:** Visa, Mastercard, Laser

NOTES:
Wheelchair access. No reservations, although you can put your name down for a table if you call in after 6pm, and they will ring you back when it's ready.

DIRECTIONS:
Fade St runs between Drury Street and South Great George's St. The restaurant is beside Hogan's Pub.

HARVEY NICHOLS

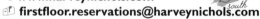

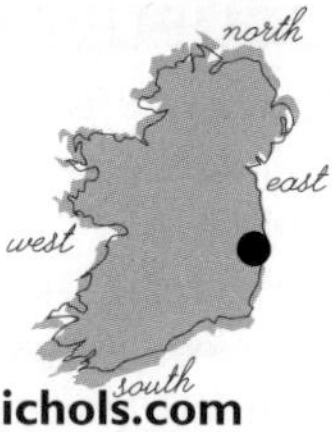

Robert Haughton
Dundrum Town Centre
Sandyford Road, Dublin 16
+353 (0) 1-291 0488
www.harveynichols.com
firstfloor.reservations@harveynichols.com

The centre is nothing but a commercial symphony, but give thanks for the grace notes of Harvey Nick's and their acute quality control and care.

In his book on Los Angeles, *City of Quartz,* Mike Davis forever dug the hole for modern shopping centres when he described them as "a veritable commercial symphony of swarming, consuming nomads moving from one cashpoint to another". Dundrum Shopping Centre how are you? Welcome to hell. But, even hell must have some respite, and in the DSC that comes in the form of Harvey Nick's restaurant and, by the by, also in its fine Espresso bar where we enjoyed some extremely nice food with the youngsters one day in late summer: spicy Moroccan meatballs with cous cous and yogurt; Thai fish stew with basmati; Cajun chicken wings with blue cheese dip; pea risotto with rocket and Parmesan. Nice food, nice room. Of course, it is their big 100-seater restaurant upstairs, where that fine chef Robert Haughton rattles the pans, that deservedly gets the maximum attention for producing fine contemporary cooking. But the Espresso bar experience was telling about the sort of quality control HN exerts, a quality control that virtually guarantees a great night out in this restaurant.

- **OPEN:** noon-3pm, 6pm-10pm Mon-Fri (till 10.30pm Fri), 12.30pm-3.30pm, 6pm-10.30pm Sat, 12pm-4pm Sun
- **PRICE:** Lunch €25, Dinner €29.50-€75
- **CREDIT CARDS:** All major cards accepted

NOTES:

Wheelchair access. Pre-theatre 6pm-7.30pm, €24-€29.50

DIRECTIONS:

In the Dundrum Shopping centre, beside Harvey Nicks.

ITSA4

Domini & Peaches Kemp
6A Sandymount Green
Dublin 4
+353 (0) 1-219 4676
www.itsabagel.com
itsa4@itsabagel.ie

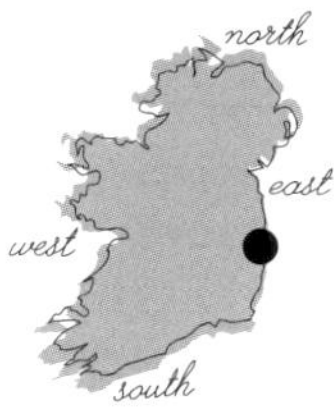

Itsa4 is a brilliant concept – an ever-accessible local restaurant – but the execution far outweighs the concept in this rigorous and splendid restaurant.

Some people thrive on multiple challenges. Having crafted the success of their Itsabagel chain, the Kemp sisters became fully-fledged restaurateurs with the marvellous Itsa4. Others might have stopped there, but they have most recently moved down to the deep south, with the opening of Table in Brown Thomas in Cork city, a slick room with good cooking.

The logistics of running so many operations would cause others to blanch, but the Kemps know how to make and motivate great crews in all their places, and they know how to make things run like clockwork. Itsa4 runs like a dream, with hip modern cooking solidly founded on the use of first-rate ingredients. These girls have no delusions of grandeur: what they do is to feed people well, in superb rooms that are a joy to be in, at prices that mean you will be back again next week. So, for tonight, let's have leg of lamb steak with hummus and pitta bread, and Terry's BBQ salmon with potato salad, and smoked haddock with lemon and mustard mash, and let's have as good a time as we had the last time, and the next time.

- **OPEN:** noon-3pm Mon-Fri, 12am-4pm Sat-Sun, 5.30pm-10pm Mon-Sat, 5pm-9pm Sun
- **PRICE:** Lunch €25, Dinner €35-€40
- **CREDIT CARDS:** Visa, Mastercard, Laser

NOTES:

Wheelchair access.
Children's menu.

DIRECTIONS:

Overlooking Sandymount Green.

LOCKS

Kelvin Rynhart & Teresa Carr
1 Windsor Terrace
Portobello, Dublin 8
+353 (0) 1-454 3391
www.locksrestaurant.ie
info@locksrestaurant.ie

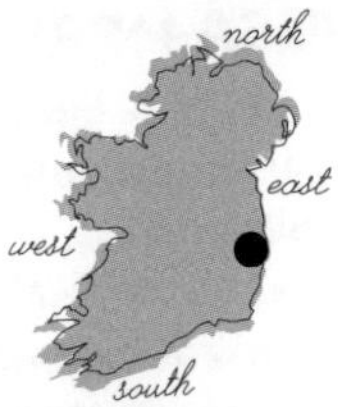

"Put simply, this is some of the finest tasting food in the country." Troy Maguire is making magic.

Our man Leslie Williams was by no means finished in describing Troy Maguire's cooking as some of the country's best.

"Every dish we ate was faultless", wrote Leslie, so here is the faultless list: Mackerel with horseradish, smoked eel, apple and fennel salad was crisply cooked mackerel with all the flavours in the salad working in harmony to lift and dignify the flavours of the fish. Duck liver and foie gras parfait with spiced pear and cornichons had depth of flavour with lightness of touch – everything a parfait should be. Fisherman's Soup had substance and heart-warming flavours. Mallard duck with Puy lentils, glazed navet, broad beans and devils on horseback was served perfectly pink and full of flavour. Dry aged rib-eye steak with bearnaise, or snail and mushroom sauce, water-cress and chips was perfection. An intense single estate chocolate brownie with kumquat and vanilla ice cream was probably the richest and most complex and perfect brownie I can remember tasting. "Bistro cooking is where it's at", Mr Maguire has said. Magic is where it's at.

- **OPEN:** noon-3pm Mon-Sat (lunch), 3pm-6pm (small bites), 6pm-10.30pm (dinner), 'till 11pm Fri & Sat. Closed Sun & bank holiday Mons
- **PRICE:** Lunch €30-€35 Dinner €50-€55
- **CREDIT CARDS:** Visa, Mastercard, Amex, Laser

- **NOTES:**

Wheelchair access, but no disabled toilet.

- **DIRECTIONS:**

In between Portobello and Harold's Cross bridges on the corner of Windsor Tce and Bloomfield Ave.

THE MERMAID CAFÉ

Ben Gorman & Mark Harrell
69/70 Dame Street
Temple Bar, Dublin 2
+353 (0) 1-670 8236
www.mermaid.ie
info@mermaid.ie

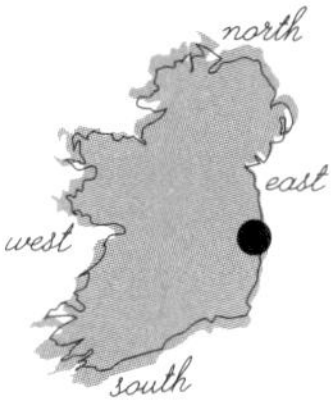

Ben and Mark's iconic Mermaid Café continues its mighty, maverick course, and remains one of the best.

It's easy today, after a decade of The Mermaid, to forget the splash this punky restaurant first made when it opened, back in the infancy of the Celtic Tiger. Ben Gorman and Mark Harrell's restaurant was – and is – a maverick: maverick cooking; maverick style; maverick ambience; maverick dynamic. It is possible to speculate that, without the Mermaid's quiet iconoclasm, the Dublin restaurant scene could well have turned out quite differently – could L'Gueuleton have been created, or The Winding Stair, or Itsa4? Future thesis writers on the Culinary Arts course at DIT will untangle this cord, but the one sure thing is that the impact and import of The Mermaid has been profound in the city.
The classics such as the fantastic crab cakes and the bounteous antipasti plate are still here, but newer riffs such as borlotti bean, ham hock and rocket soup, or veal escalope with tapenade potatoes show an almost Fergus Henderson-like relish in their upfront flavours. This isn't quite lip-smackin' food, but it has a totally distinct savour and richness, and it is always a profound, rich pleasure.

OPEN: 12.30pm-2.30pm, 6pm-10.30pm Mon-Fri; 6pm-11pm Sat, noon-3.30pm, 6pm-9pm Sun
PRICE: Lunch €25.95-€29.95, Dinner €45-€50
CREDIT CARDS: Visa, Mastercard, Amex, Laser

NOTES:
Wheelchair access. Reservations recommended.

DIRECTIONS:
Dame Street runs from Trinity College up to Christchurch, and The Mermaid is half way up, beside the Olympia Theatre.

MINT

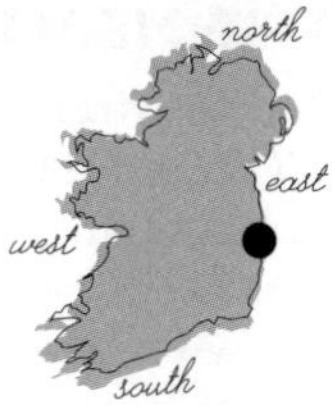

Patricia Courtney
47 Ranelagh Village
Dublin 6
+353 (0) 1-497 8655
www.mintrestaurant.ie
info@mintrestaurant.ie

Dylan McGreath's cooking has no precise parallel in Dublin, a whirlwind of culinary intensity that has to be experienced.

It is the fact that Dylan McGrath has won the praise of his fellow professional chefs for his cooking at Mint that tells you all you need to know about one of the hottest new talents to have emerged in Dublin in recent times. When we quote people talking about "3-star cooking" it isn't McGrath's customers we are quoting: it is other top chefs who have found themselves blown away by the sheer excitement of the food he is producing. "I want to get buckets of flavour onto the plate and I won't apologise for that", McGrath once told our man Leslie Williams, and buckets of pure, concentrated, focused flavours are what you get throughout the whirlygig of the seven-course tasting menu, with main ingredients counterpointed by grace notes such as saffron with roasted seabass; pear purée with pigeon; celeriac lasagne with pig head; beetroot foam with marinated salmon; red wine foam and jelly with vanilla pannacotta. This cooking is great to eat, but also great to think, as McGrath works a series of inspired themes and variations on superb ingredients.

- **OPEN:** 6.30pm-10pm Tue-Sat; 12.30pm-2.20pm Fri
- **PRICE:** Lunch €35-€43, Dinner Tasting menu €105
- **CREDIT CARDS:** Visa, Mastercard, Laser, Amex

● NOTES:

Wheelchair access. Open for lunch during the month of Dec, Tue-Sat

● DIRECTIONS:

Opposite the 24-hour Spar, next to the Kelli boutique, and right smack in the centre of Ranelagh village.

NONNA VALENTINA

Stefano Crescenzi & Eileen Dunne
1-2 Portobello Road,
Dublin 6
+353 (0) 1-454 9866
www.dunneandcrescenzi.com
dunneandcrescenzi@hotmail.com

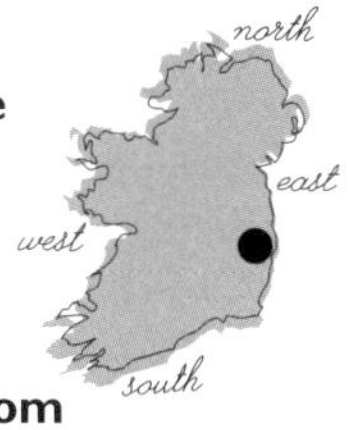

Stefano Crescenzi's cooking makes the tradition seem freshly conceived, thanks to its particularity, passion and quiet, disciplined perfection.

"I now had a metaphor for the type of cooking that made sense to me: food grounded in a tradition, yet enlivened by the act of greeting the process and the ingredients anew".
The Italian-American chef Paul Bertolli's statement of discovering his true metier, in his book *Cooking by Hand*, could act as a definition and decription of the "curato" style of Italian food produced by Stefano Crescenzi, in Nonna Valentina. Mr Crescenzi's cooking is simple, seemingly, and yet it is depthless, inspired by generations of cooks, not least Mr Crescenzi's grandmother. Reading the dishes on the menu – pasta filled with mushrooms and sheep's cheese with guinea fowl jus; fettuccine with wild hare sauce; venison with aged balsamic and juniper; guinea fowl with porcini mushroom sauce – gives no clue to the intensity of flavours conjured up here by slow, patient creation of intense sauces counterpointed by pillow light pasta and the toothy countrpoint of main ingredients. Nonna Valentina gives us tradition enlivened by a new greeting, and it's a pure, pure thrill.

- **OPEN:** noon-10.30pm Mon-Wed & Sun, noon-11pm Thu-Sat
- **PRICE:** Lunch €25-€30, Dinner €40
- **CREDIT CARDS:** All major cards accepted

- **NOTES:**

Full wheelchair access. Corporate menu noon-3pm, pre-theatre menu 4pm-7pm, €22.50. No cheques.

- **DIRECTIONS:**

On the banks of the canal in between the Portobello and Harold's Cross bridges.

O'CONNELL'S

Tom O'Connell
@ Bewley's Hotel, Merrion Rd
Ballsbridge, Dublin 4
+353 (0) 1-647 3304
www.oconnellsballsbridge.com
info@oconnellsballsbridge.com

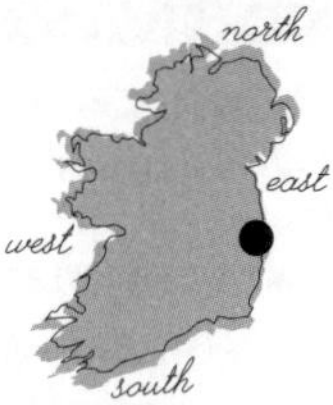

Dublin's great restaurateur continues to tweak, refine, improve and better the offer in the brilliant O'Connell's.

The menus in O'Connell's put us in mind of those fine old expansive menus that were once the staple of hotel dining rooms. Salads. Soups. Seafood. Pasta, Pizza & Vegetarian Dishes. Bakes, Roasts & Grills. Fish. Little Desserts. An entire culinary world assembled for your delectation, served in a lovely room by dedicated stiff. My God, we could be on board The Queen Mary! Where's my dinner jacket! Polish my shoes!

There is no other restaurant proprietor like Tom O'Connell, no one else with so little ego and such expansive capacity for hard work and innovation. O'Connell's has been pretty perfect from day one, but Mr O'Connell never ceases to tweak and improve, to better and to offer more – most recently it's been the introduction of breakfast on Saturday morning, before that it was the revising of the Sunday lunch offer. The room has also been painted to intoduce more colour, more softness. The analogy with a cruise liner is not inappropriate, for if you had to eat breakfast, lunch and dinner in O'Connell's it would be sheer bliss in Dublin.

● **OPEN:** 7am-10.30am, noon-2.30pm, 5.30pm-10pm Mon-Sat. (Sat breakfast from 7.30am-11am). 8am-11am, 12.45pm-3.30pm, 5.30pm-9.30pm Sun
● **PRICE:** Lunch €23.75, Dinner €32
● **CREDIT CARDS:** All major cards accepted.

● **NOTES:**
Wheelchair access. Early bird menu €21.25-€25.25

● **DIRECTIONS:**
Basement of Bewley's Hotel on Merrion Rd.

101 TALBOT

Margaret Duffy & Pascal Bradley
101 Talbot Street
Dublin 1
+353 (0) 1-874 5011
www.101talbot.com

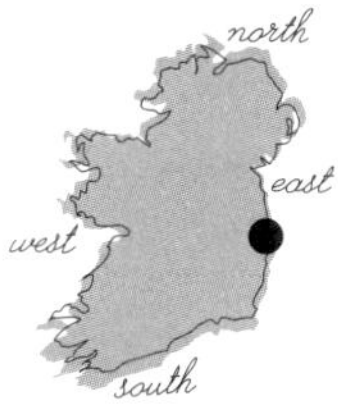

"You go up a simple staircase and open the door on what seems like the best party in town", says Valerie O'Connor. That's 101 Talbot all right.

"I had pathetic intentions of having a light meal but chose the Crispy Pork Belly wrapped in Savoy Cabbage served with a plum and ginger sauce as my starter. It was a joy to behold on the plate", writes Valerie. So, what else was good in 101? "Warm duck liver salad with roast pine-nut and balsamic dressing was very rare and deliciously tender, almost runny in the middle. Char-grilled Swordfish with smoked garlic and chilli butter came with its butter running down its sides. It was juicy and delicious, falling apart at the touch of my fork. The smoked garlic butter had none of the usual tang of garlic butter and didn't murder the fish's delicate flavours. The star of the show was the pan roast venison served with sautéed bacon and cabbage and redcurrant jus. The venison, cooked to medium was melt in the mouth and so rich. Dark chocolate cheesecake with strawberries was one of those ones that make you cry, it was so rich and dense it almost crumbled, and "oohs" and "aahs" could be heard from other diners in the same state of bliss who had ordered it." All well in 101 Talbot.

- **OPEN:** 5pm-11pm Tue-Sat
- **PRICE:** Dinner €30
- **CREDIT CARDS:** All major cards accepted

NOTES:

Reservations recommended at weekends. Recommended for vegetarians. Early bird, 5pm-7.30pm €21.50. No wheelchair access.

DIRECTIONS:

3 minutes' walk from the Dublin Spire.

POULOT'S

Jean-Michel & Lorna-Jean Poulot
Mulberry Gardens, Donnybrook
Dublin 4
+353 (0) 1-269 3300
www.poulots.ie
poulotjm@eircom.net

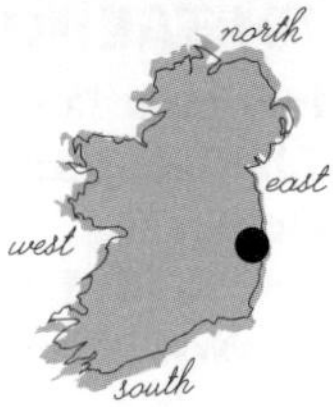

Comfortable and comforting in a quietly clamorous way, Poulot's is one of the best destinations for business, and for the fine business of romance.

Jean-Michel and Lorna-Jean Poulot are already into the award-garnering game, after only a year or so in Poulot's, their chic, comfy restaurant set back just off the main strip of Donnybrook.Their team work is a match made in heaven – he one of the city's most experienced chefs, she a talented and expert sommelier. In addition to the day-to-day business of running this handsome restaurant, they have also begun to offer six-week cookery and wine courses, a logical outreach of their respective skills. But, for diners, their respective skills come most vividly to the fore in their daily work. Poulot's is a glam, slick, polished palette of a restaurant experience, a place that seems to have been invented for the serious business lunch and the seriously romantic dinner.Whilst M. Poulot loves Asian food, he never mixes things up on the one plate: rabbit loin has a Pommery mustard cream and Puy lentils; tuna sashimi has sticky rice and pickled vegetables, and the European classics concepts are never confused with his Asian sorties. Helpful wine suggestions ally with the menu's offerings, the result is pure class.

● **OPEN:** 12.30pm-2.30pm Tue-Fri, 7pm-10.30pm Tue-Sat
● **PRICE:** Lunch €28.50-€35, Dinner €55-€60
● **CREDIT CARDS:** All major cards accepted

● **NOTES:**
Wheelchair access. 8-course tasting menu, 7pm-8.30pm, €75

● **DIRECTIONS:**
In the centre of Donnybrook village, go through the laneway beside Kiely's pub.

THE SILK ROAD CAFÉ

Ibraham Phelan
Chester Beatty Museum
Dublin Castle, Dublin 2
+353 (0) 1-407 0770
www.silkroadcafe.ie
silkroadcafe@hotmail.com

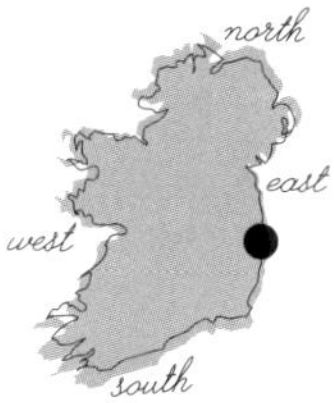

Ibraham Phelan is producing some of the city's best ethnic cooking, but make sure to get there early to enjoy the best of the Silk Road Café.

Sally McKenna hadn't even finishd her lunchtime dish of lamb and vegetable moussaka with mung bean and pea salad, tadziki and mint and lemon zest before she said "This is 100 Best cooking!". And so it is. The Silk Road, tucked away beside the fabulous Chester Beatty Library in the bowels of Dublin Castle, may well be the best-kept secret in Dublin, but it sure isn't going to stay that way for long. Ibraham Phelan had attracted attention when cooking at the mosque out in Clonskeagh, and here in the city he is firing out sublime food.

The cooking takes mainly-Mediterranean ideas – lamb curry with chickpeas; pizza; spinach pie; stir-fried lamb; moussaka – and to this Mr Phelan weaves a Middle Eastern array of seasonings and grace notes which gives the food distinctiveness and very pleasing textures – the food is particularly light, and expertly seasoned, which goes a long way to explaining how it attracts such a hip crowd of punters. Do be warned that you need to arrive early at lunchtime to make sure you get a seat, and it gets very busy when there are big exhibitions in the CB.

- **OPEN:** 10am-4.30pm Tue-Fri, 11am-4.30pm Sat, 1pm-4.30pm Sun
- **PRICE:** Lunch €12
- **CREDIT CARDS:** Visa, Mastercard, Laser

NOTES:
Wheelchair access. Outside catering available.

DIRECTIONS:
In the Chester Beatty Library, just behind Dublin Castle.

10 GREAT

SIGNATURE DISHSES

1

Bon Appetit: Boudin of Skate & braised Pork Belly with Girole purée & crispy capers

2

Fallon & Byrne: Milk-poached belly of Pork Clove Red Cabbage

3

The Farm Gate: Corned Beef with Colcannon

4

Fishy Fishy Café: Skate wing with Samphire, Chanterelles, fennel salad

5

Good Things Café: Ham Sandwich

6

Locks: Mallard Duck with Puy Lentils, glazed Navet, Broad Beans & Devils on Horseback

7

Out of the Blue: Turbot Cutlet with its own Foie Gras, smoked Roe, Morels, violet Mustard cream

8

Silk Road Café: Lamb Curry with Chickpeas Rice, Sticky Tomato Ratatouille

9

The Tannery Restaurant: Crab Crème Brulée

10

The Winding Stair: Collar Bacon with organic Cabbage & Parsley Sauce

RASAM

Nisheeth Tak
Eagle Pub, 18/19 Glasthule Road
Glasthule, County Dublin
+353 (0) 1-230 0600
www.rasam.ie
info@rasam.ie

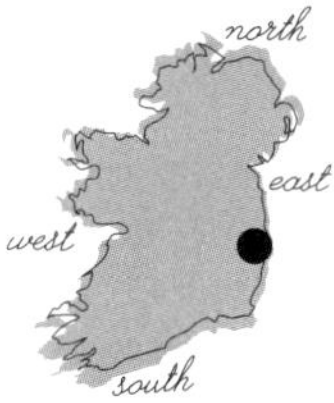

Exemplary execution and beautiful presentation of true cuisine in a lovely room mark out Rasam.

Nisheeth Tak has been living and working in Ireland since 1990, bringing his management brilliance, and his determination to serve the true cooking of India, to an Irish audience. In Rasam, he may well be doing his best work ever, with a crack team under chefs Avinash Mohan and Sanjay Vishwakarma.
The kitchen have left behind the ersatz curry house blandness in favour of dishes that explore regional themes and seasonings, so you can travel from the beaches of Mumbai to the Punjab or Pondicherry and onto Kashmir, taking in street food and tiffin cooking, all within the delicious ambit of a series of dishes shared at dinner. As with any great cooking, it is attention to detail that singles out Rasam: the orange powder and fenugreek used in their version of chicken tikka masala, the tamarind bite of prawns with mustard seeds in karavali jhinga, the use of patthar ke phool spicing in their lamb varuval. There are helpful suggestions as to what side dishes to choose, and there are some old classics for the timid, but Rasam is the place for culinary adventure.

- **OPEN:** 5.30pm-11pm Mon-Sun
- **PRICE:** Dinner €45
- **CREDIT CARDS:** Visa, Mastercard, Laser

- **NOTES:**

Early bird menu, 5.30pm-7pm Sun-Thur, €21.95

- **DIRECTIONS:**
- **DIRECTIONS:**

Over the Eagle pub in the centre of Glasthule.

THORNTON'S

Kevin & Muriel Thornton
St. Stephen's Green
Dublin 2
+353 (0) 1-478 7008
www.thorntonsrestaurant.com
thorntonsrestaurant@eircom.net

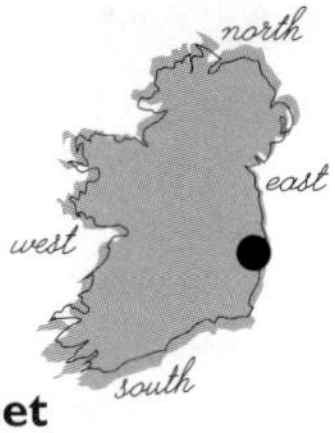

Back in the saddle with a revamped room and a canapé bar, Thornton's has the wind in its sails again.

There is a new energy evident in Thornton's. With a revamped restaurant interior, a new canapé bar where you can graze on delicately delicious small eats and glasses of wine at really keen prices, Kevin Thornton's restaurant has gotten back to the mantra of excellence-for-everyone which has characterised his work over the years. Thornton has said that he draws inspiration from people like Patti Smith and Louis le Brocquy, and it's not in the slightest bit fanciful both to compare him to these singular artists, and to suggest that his cooking may have entered a new artistic phase, just as Le Brocquy's work shows endless mutations, and as Patti Smith's has veered from one artistic pivot to the next. Certainly, the colours, textures and flavours which Thornton brings to his work evoke endless artistic comparisons, but ultimately his cooking is its own thing, "a style that you can recognise immediately" as the critic Marco Bolasco has written. Prepare for extraordinary combinations, such as sea urchins, trotters and sweetbreads, but above all prepare to have a great time, great fun, and great food.

- **OPEN:** 12.30pm-2pm, 7pm-10.30pm Tue-Sat
- **PRICE:** Lunch €35-€45, Dinner €85-€180
- **CREDIT CARDS:** All major cards accepted

NOTES:

Full wheelchair access.
Recommended for vegetarians.

DIRECTIONS:

In the centre of Dublin, on the west side of St Stephen's Green. The restaurant has an entrance at the side of the Fitzwilliam Hotel.

TOWN BAR & GRILL

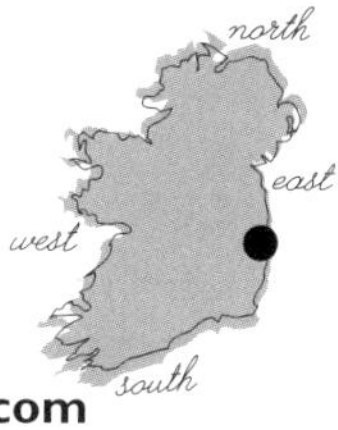

Temple Garner & Ronan Ryan
21 Kildare Street
Dublin 2
+353 (0) 1-662 4724
www.townbarandgrill.com
reservations@townbarandgrill.com

Town-South-Bridge. That's the Ronan Ryan and Temple Garner trilogy of Dublin eating rooms. Next? Well, it has to be Country, surely?

Having opened the big, 200-seater South at the Beacon Centre in Sandyford, in addition to running the red-hot Town in centre city, chef Temple Garner and f-o-h Ronan Ryan are not yet ready to call a halt to their plans to expand. The latest project is a 78-seater bistro, Bridge Bar & Grill, at Barrow Street in Ringsend near the Gasworks, planned to open just as this book hits the shelves.
This sort of growth, typical of Avoca under Simon Pratt, or Ely under Erik Robson, or Deane's under Michael Deane, shows the measure of these blokes – they are not only talented restaurateurs, but also talented business operators, mimicking the model of such Stateside luminaries as Danny Meyer or Wolfgang Puck.
But, with their other operations in their infancy, we still give Town the top rating, a great room with big, big flavoured cooking – sort of New York Italian, if you like, meaning that it draws on those sources for energy more than for a template of tastes, and brings a dash of operatic grandeur to both – and the sort of energy that is utterly seductive, utterly metropolitan, utterly now.

- **OPEN:** 12.30pm-11pm Mon-Sat; 12.30pm-10pm Sun
- **PRICE:** Lunch €22.95-€27.95, Dinner €50
- **CREDIT CARDS:** Visa, Mastercard, Amex

NOTES:
No wheelchair access. Health-conscious low-sodium kid's menu. €9.95. Pre-theatre menu Mon-Thur, 5.30pm-7pm €29.95.

DIRECTIONS:
In the basement of Mitchell's Wine Cellars.

VENU BRASSERIE

Charles Guilbaud
Anne's Lane
Dublin 2
+353 (0) 1-670 6755
www.venu.ie

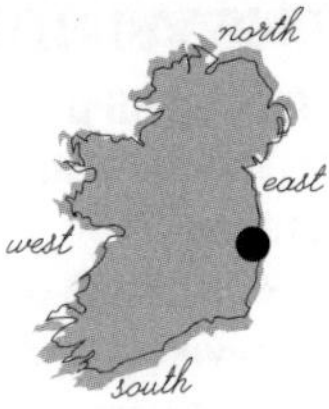

Rock-steady brasserie cooking, that respects and reinvents the great French dishes we all love has made Venu a rock-steady Dublin destination.

"I think Venu has no bad dishes", says Leslie Williams, quite a statement when you consider the weight of history that rests upon the menu selection in Charles Guilbaud's basement brasserie.
Ageless classics such as onion soup; terrine of duck foie gras; traditional fish and chips; beef in red wine sauce; lobster with garlic butter; bread and butter pudding, are such venerable mainstays that they almost invite you to recall comparisons eaten either recently, or in the distant past, locally or internationally, and it really does say something about the Venu venture that they chose these dishes, and have stuck with getting them right and doing them right, day in, day out.
As Leslie also points out, referring to their dish of grilled lamb skewer with cumin and coriander spices, served with grilled courgettes in a yogurt and lime sauce, "This did exactly what it said on the tin, and was very well executed with every piece of lamb perfectly charred on the outside and perfectly pink in the middle". Venu is good at doing, and delivering, what they say on the tin.

- **OPEN:** noon-11pm
- **PRICE:** Lunch €20, Dinner €38
- **CREDIT CARDS:** Visa, Mastercard, Amex

- **NOTES:**

Wheelchair access.
Bar open noon-12.30am

- **DIRECTIONS:**

Anne's Lane runs off South Anne Street, which leads onto Dublin's main shopping street, Grafton Street.

THE WINDING STAIR

Elaine Murphy
40 Lower Ormond Quay
Dublin 1
+353 (0) 1-872 7320
www.winding-stair.com
restaurant@winding-stair.com

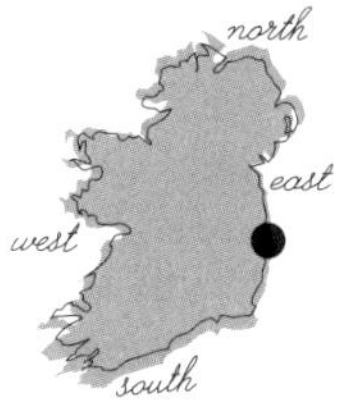

One of the most exciting new arrivals on Dublin's pulsing scene, the Winding Stair is a culinary home from home.

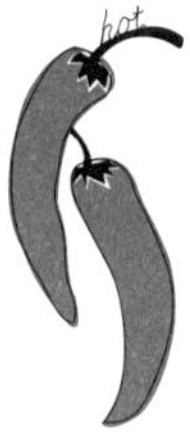

Aoife Carrigy of *Food & Wine* magazine has described the re-incarnation of the iconic Winding Stair as being "the most exciting" of Dublin's many recent restaurant arrivals, and she hit the nail on the head by saying that "this riverside building deserved the kind of team that now call it home". With manager Elaine Murphy and chef Aine Maguire squeezing out culinary sparks with their inspired new Irish cooking, the WS has indeed got the crew it demanded. This isn't just another restaurant: this is one of those restaurants that expresses the zeitgeist of both the culinary culture and the city culture, and that is no mean feat. Ms Maguire's impeccably sourced and beautifully curated cooking is inspiring: potted Kerry crab with soda bread; Gubbeen chorizo with white clam chowder and dilisk bread; collar bacon with organic cabbage and parsley sauce; Irish charcuterie board; field mushrooms with Bellingham Blue; bread and butter pudding with whiskey sauce. This is cooking to sustain a nation, and the kind of restaurant that you will think of as home from home.

- **OPEN:** 12.30pm-3.30pm Mon-Sun, 6pm-10.30pm Tue-Sat, 6pm-9.30pm Sun
- **PRICE:** Lunch & Dinner €40
- **CREDIT CARDS:** Visa, Mastercard

NOTES:
No wheelchair access.

DIRECTIONS:
The Winding Stair faces directly on to the Ha'penny bridge on the north side of the River Liffey in central Dublin.

WINE NOT

1 Coliemore Road,
Dalkey
County Dublin
+ 353 (0) 1-235 2988
winenot@eircom.net

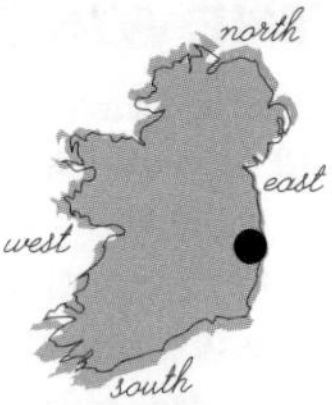

A hip address where great Italian cooking and superb Italian wines are married together in bliss.

Winenot is so utterly hip it is almost embarrassing. The staff all seem to not only have PhDs in service and wine selection, they have also clearly worked harvests making Sassicaia, and been plongeurs for Carlo Cracco. So, take our advice in Winenot, place yourself in their hands – gently! – and let the evening flow as they choose the wines and decide which of the evening's dishes would best complement the gorgeous Italian wines.

So, is Winenot more a wine-with-food place more than a food-with-wine place? No. The balance here between the expertise of the food and the sheer lusciousness of the wines is well balanced, so you eat very well and drink very well. That fennel salad with red snapper is precisely right, and the note of mandarin orange and caper berry that fans out the flavour of the dish is perfect. With pastas, they show exactly how to make the right sauce – concentrated, pure, intense – and they know to serve just the correct – small – amount with excellent fresh pasta. The desire to keep flavours clear, and wine compatible, is happily everywhere, and Winenot is fab.

- **OPEN:** 5.30pm-10.30pm Tue-Thu, 5.30pm-11pm Fri & Sat, 4pm-9.30pm Sun
- **PRICE:** Dinner €36, Sun menu €20.95-€23.95
- **CREDIT CARDS:** Visa,

NOTES:
Early Bird Menu 5.30pm-7.30pm Mon-Sun, €20.95-€23.95

DIRECTIONS:
In the centre of Dalkey village.

ARD BIA & ARD BIA @ NIMMOS

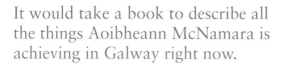

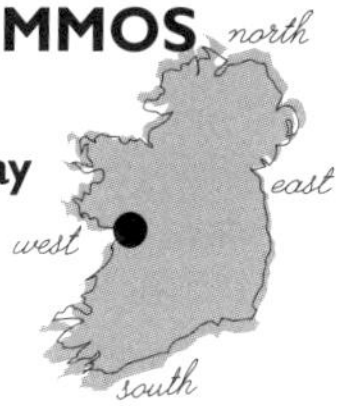

Aoibheann McNamara
● Spanish Arch, Long Walk, Galway
+353 (0) 91-561 114
● 2 Quay Street, Galway
+353 (0) 91-539 897
www.ardbia.com
ardbia@gmail.com

It would take a book to describe all the things Aoibheann McNamara is achieving in Galway right now.

It would take a book, not just a single entry, to describe what Aoibheann McNamara is achieving in the pair of Ard Bias. But we can get to the essence of the woman by quoting this remark she made in *The Irish Times*: "Food that is made with love is what the Indians call prana – living energy. That's what we aspire to".
That's not just what they aspire to: that is what they achieve, most recently with the new restaurant in the lovely old Nimmo's. Warm brie and pistachio organic salad; crab pots with crusty bread; pan-fried turbot with spring onion mash and vegetable stew; corn-fed chicken in yogurt dressing with couscous. The food is rustic, and this atmospheric restaurant, with its bricolage style, is a cracker. At the central Ard Bia, the food is just as intricately conceived and complex, yet direct, as Ms McNamara herself. Two utterly brilliant Galway destinations.

● **OPEN:** Nimmos open 6pm-10.30pm Tue-Sun (downstairs), 7pm-10.30pm Fri & Sat during high season only (upstairs). Ard Bia Café open 10am-5pm Mon-Sat; noon-5pm Sun. Restaurant open 6.30pm-10.30pm Tue-Sat
● **PRICE:** Nimmos menu €38, Nimmos Upstairs €50 Ard Bia Cafe lunch €6-€12, Dinner €42
● **CREDIT CARDS:** Visa, Mastercard, Laser, Amex

● **NOTES:**
Wheelchair access, but no disabled toilet in Nimmos. Nimmos Supper club and private functions upstairs. Ard Bia Cookery courses & Art Gallery

● **DIRECTIONS:**
Galway city centre.

KAPPA-YA

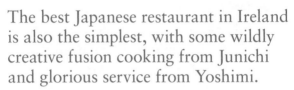

Yoshimi Hayakawa & Junichi Yoshiyagawa
5 Middle Street, Galway
County Galway
+353 (0) 86-3543616

The best Japanese restaurant in Ireland is also the simplest, with some wildly creative fusion cooking from Junichi and glorious service from Yoshimi.

It is hard to resist the feeling, in the middle of a spell-binding dinner in Kappa-Ya, that you are witnessing, and enjoying, some of the most naturally and spontaneously evolving fusion cooking that anyone has ever created in Ireland. When Junichi presents a dish like lamb Kappa-Ya, where miso and Cashel Blue cheese are brought together with grilled lamb, then you really do go outside the box of conventional, or expected, flavours, into something completely new.
The thrill is not just new tastes and textures: it is the fact of the new culinary logics and possibilities that are being created that is so dazzling.
Best of all, this is fusion created out of experiment and necessity, and not from gratuitous grandstanding. When Junichi cannot get an ingredient to make a dish in the conventionl Japanese way, then he goes foraging for the new, and it means Kappa-Ya just has to be tried. It also has to be tried because of Yoshimi's graceful, charming service, and for the fact that the simplicity of the room is one of those things that makes Galway "Galway".

- **OPEN:** noon-6.30pm Mon-Fri. Dinner by reservation only, one week's notice.
- **PRICE:** Lunch €10 per dish
- **CREDIT CARDS:** Visa, Mastercard, Laser

NOTES:
Wheelchair access, but no disabled toilet. Recommended for children. Miso soup and sushi to take away. Lunch menu served 'till 4pm.

DIRECTIONS:
Middle Street is between High St and St. Augustine Pl.

OSCAR'S

Michael O'Meara & Sinead Hughes
Upper Dominick St, Galway
County Galway
+353 (0) 91-582180
www.oscarsgalway.com

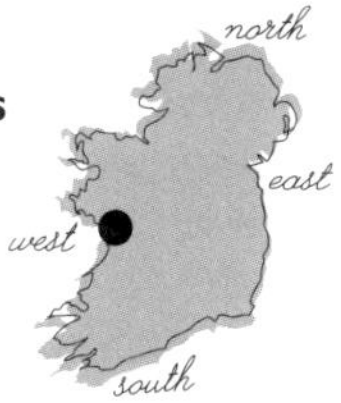

O'Meara and Hughes might sound like a firm of Galway solicitors, but in fact it's the crack team behind Galway's inimitable Oscar's restaurant.

Michael O'Meara is fast becoming one of the major West Coast culinary players. His restaurant hauls in awards for his iconoclastic and fascinating cooking – everything from chicken yakitori to tarragon frog's legs, from plaice Bonaparte to salmon with mung beans, from Mexican fajitas to prawn and chilli sambal – and his wife, Sinead Hughes, is as acclaimed for her service as her husband is for his funky cooking.

But Mr O'Meara is also a player in the Galway Food Group, a bunch of committed food lovers and professionals who aim to improve the ambit and compass of food in and around this extraordinary city. And it this double pincer of activity that will bring Mr O'Meara, and his unique restaurant, to greater attention.

In the meantime, however, there is much to be enjoyed in Oscar's, not least its wild style of decoration – there really is no other room in Ireland quite like this, a space that looks like it has been parachuted in from some wild club in Barcelona. But Oscar's is not just some wild show: it is the work of two intellectual, creative people.

- **OPEN:** 7pm-late Mon-Fri, 6pm-late Sat
- **PRICE:** Dinner €45
- **CREDIT CARDS:** Visa, Mastercard, Laser

- **NOTES:**

Wheelchair access, but no disabled toilet.

- **DIRECTIONS:**

Cross the bridge at Jury's, and follow the road past Monroes Tavern, the restaurant is across the street from Roisin Dubh bar.

PANGUR BÁN

John Walsh & Mairead Tucker
Letterfrack, Connemara
County Galway
+353 (0) 95-41243
www.pangurban.com
pban@indigo.ie

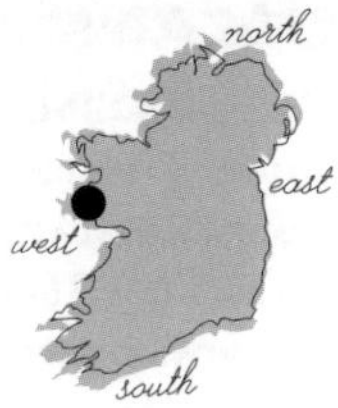

A true Connemara solid-sender, John and Mairead's stone cottage restaurant may look rustic, but there is a very modern sensibility at work here.

He is a funky cook, John Walsh, but his experience means that his fusion notes sound – and taste – sweet, rather than sharp or bitter. Sometimes he adds a delicate note to a dish – chilli butter with salmon, a good mix; apricots in a curry with venison, a fruit and meat combo that few cooks could pull off convincingly, indeed something few chef would even dream of doing. His cooking puts us in mind of Abstract Expressionism: it's from the heart, with vivid techniques used, to create something that is quite distinctive.
The Jackson Pollock of the kitchen, then?No, not quite. Mr Walsh's sensibility is curious rather than anarchic, and he is a traveller rather than a culinary renegade. Fish taco with salsa will be on the same menu with pheasant and duck liver terrine with Melba toast; pheasant with port sauce will be on offer beside jardiloo boti – a lamb curry – with naan bread. Indeed, the most iconoclastic thing about this pretty stone cottage restaurant is the unpredicability of the menus, but there is nothing unpredictable about the assurance of the cooking or service.

- **OPEN:** 6pm-9.30pm, Mon-Sun high-season. Limited hours mid and low season; phone to check. Closed Nov, mid Jan-mid Mar
- **PRICE:** Dinner €40-€45
- **CREDIT CARDS:** Visa, Mastercard, Laser

NOTES:

Full wheelchair access. Booking essential, especially high season. Cookery classes Mar-May & Sept-Oct

DIRECTIONS:

Opposite the Connemara National Park.

BIALANN & SEOMRAÍ SÓ INIS MEÁIN

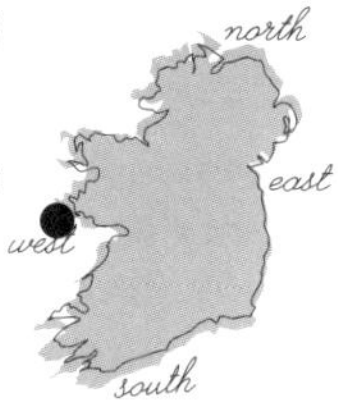

Ruairi & Marie-Therese de Blacam
Inis Meain, Aran Islands,
+353 (0) 86-826 6026
www.inismeain.com
post@inismeain.com

A new arrival on the most beautiful of the Aran Islands, Bialann só Inis Meáin is a new star.

If you had asked us how we would go about regenerating the reputation of the Aran Islands as a 5-star destination, we would have said: build a beautiful resturant with rooms on Inis Meain, and have it cook island ingredients with simplicity and panache. Ruairi and Marie-Therese de Blacam never asked us. They just went ahead and did it anyway. And they did it much better than we could ever have imagined.

It helps to have the luminary firm of de Blacam and Meagher Architects as one element of the family, and the new building is as great an architectural triumph as the firm created with Shanks in Northern Ireland. To this triumphant template the de Blacams bring a style of service and a style of food that is utterly comfortable in its skin: fresh crab with the tiniest dice of mango and fresh leaves. Oven-baked cod with lobster bisque and the greenest broad beans. Beautiful grilled chicken with carrots and fennel. Island potatoes still in their skins, slathered with butter. The purity of the cooking, its modesty and timelessness, is sublime, and inspiring.

- **OPEN:** Seasonally, ring to check
- **PRICE:** Dinner €45
- **CREDIT CARDS:** Visa, Mastercard, Laser

- **NOTES:**

Take ferry from Rosaveal, or the plane from Inverin. Three accommodation suites, €100 per person B&B

- **DIRECTIONS:**

In the middle of the village past the pub as you come from the pier.

THE CHART HOUSE

Jim & Carmel McCarthy
The Mall, Dingle
County Kerry
+353 (0) 66-915 2255
www.thecharthousedingle.com
charthse@iol.ie

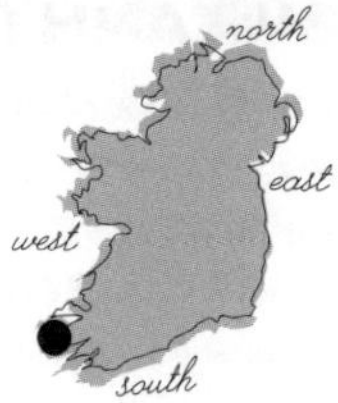

McCarthy and Enright are the culinary equivalent of Kerry football legends Cooper and Donaghy.

"Ten out of 10" was how *The Irish Times* energetically summarised a recent dinner in Jim and Carmel McCarthy's Chart House restaurant, where chef Noel Enright has been doing the magic for the last few years. In fact, The 'Times effectively gave Mr Enright "Eleven out of 10", because the meal was decribed as "one of the best meals of all time". Blimey.

So, how do you hit the Perfect 10, or the beyond-perfect 11? It's actually simple. You take meticulous care to source good Kerry ingredients – in particular Blasket Island lamb, and the wonderful Maharees carrots grown in the sandy soil, and the unique Annascaul Black pudding from several miles up the road – and you cook these local Kerry ingredients with skill, respect and TLC, and you get Mr McCarthy to serve them with his winning enthusiasm, and then you get "one of the best meals of all time". That's how. McCarthy and Enright are as deadly a pair of finishers as the deadly Kerry footballers Gooch Cooper and Kieran Donaghy, and they are not just local heroes: they are the All Stars of the Irish culinary team.

- **OPEN:** 6.30pm-10pm Mon-Sun Jun-Sept. (restricted hours off season, and restaurant closes 7 Jan-Valentine's Day)
- **PRICE:** Dinner €38
- **CREDIT CARDS:** Visa, Mastercard, Laser

- **NOTES:**

Wheelchair access. Value menu, dinner €35

- **DIRECTIONS:**

Directly at the roundabout, on the left-hand side, as you approach Dingle from the Killarney direction.

MULCAHY'S

Bruce Mulcahy
36 Henry Street
Kenmare
County Kerry
+353 (0) 64-42383

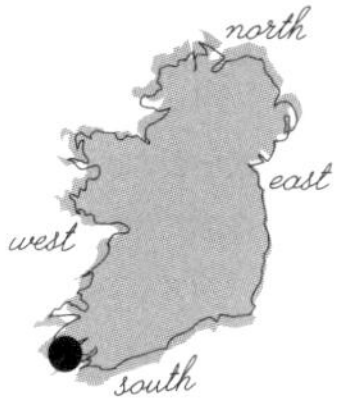

Delicious modern riffing on culinary ideas, both new and classic, are meat and drink for Mulcahy's style.

"A classic modern Irish restaurant with modern Irish cooking" is how we summed up Bruce Mulcahy's fine place in the latest Bridgestone Irish Food Guide.
But, in fact, we were wrong.
That should have read "A classic modern Irish restaurant with classic modern Irish cooking", for Mr Mulcahy is one of those cooks able to take modern benchmark Irish dishes – crab crème brulée, to take one example, – and to make them both a statement of the art, and a statement of his own style.
His cooking is persuasive, and grows ever more mature, especially since he toned down the fusion elements that were once manifest in his work. Today, things are more direct, with delicious riffing on favoured products: duck with sweet potato gratin and shallots; black sole with brown butter sauce; lamb with smoked lentils and lamb shank tart; chocolate fondant with bitter chocolate ice cream. There is balance and integrity in this cooking, and it is served by charming staff in a delightful modern room at prices that offer excellent value for such craft.

● **OPEN:** 6pm-10pm Mon-Sun (closed Tue & Wed off-season)
● **PRICE:** Dinner from €35
● **CREDIT CARDS:** All major cards accepted.

● **NOTES:**
Wheelchair access. Early bird menu served 6pm-7pm, high season only, €32.

● **DIRECTIONS:**
On the right-hand side as you travel down the one-way street, coming from Glengarriff.

OUT OF THE BLUE

Tim Mason
Waterside, Dingle
County Kerry
+353 (0) 66-915 0811
www.outoftheblue.ie
info@outoftheblue.ie

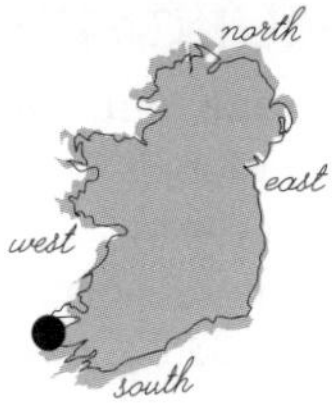

A first-class kitchen treating the catch of the day with maximum respect, OOTB is one of the hottest destinations.

Tim Mason has assembled a top-notch crew in OOTB, with sous-chef Seamus McDonald succeeding former head chef Jean-Marie Vireau, and proving that this Hebridean islander is a mighty talent who deserves close attention as his career develops. Mr McDonald is already making some mighty exciting food, and for a young chef he has a polished, personal style: a summertime lunch began with a perfectly cooked fillet of sea bass with lemon butter sauce and tapenade, before a classic dish of turbot cutlet with its own foie gras – served on a toasted crouton – and with its roe firstly smoked and then served inside poached morels, with the dish finished with a violet mustard cream. This is grandstanding cooking, and yet the perfect alliance of all the fish ingredients, and the inherent, wise economy of the dish, reveal modesty rather than any arrogance. It is this sympathetic modesty that has made OOTB such a winner in Dingle: their calling is to treat their fish and shellfish with maximum respect and concern, and this aim they achieve with enormous success.

- **OPEN:** 12.30pm-3pm, 6.30pm-9.30pm Mon-Sat; noon-3pm, 6pm-8.30pm Sun. Open every day except Wed. Closed Nov-Feb open wed night high season
- **PRICE:** Lunch €14-€18, Dinner €45
- **CREDIT CARDS:** Visa, Mastercard, Laser

NOTES:

Wheelchair access to front table in shop. Wine Bar now open. Restaurant closes if they run out of fish.

DIRECTIONS:

Directly opposite the main pier in Dingle.

PACKIE'S

Martin Hallissey
Henry Street
Kenmare
County Kerry
+353 (0) 64-41508

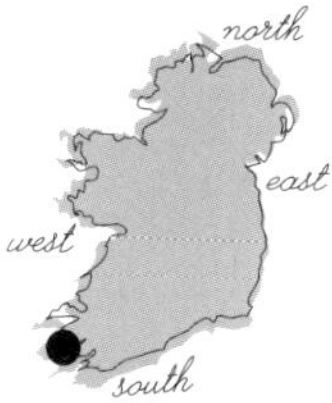

The Packie's experience is one of the quintessential Kerry experiences: sublime restaurant, amazing food.

Martin Hallissey has one of the best crews, working both in the kitchen and front-of-house, that you will find anywhere in Ireland.The team create what can only be described as a true "Kerry"experience in Packie's: the service is maternal yet never slack nor slick, just patently polite, and endlessly solicitous, dedicated to making sure that you have a great time.

The kitchen crew then produce cooking that echoes this splendidly atmospheric service – light, flaky crab cake with tartare sauce; potato pancakes with garlic butter; seafood sausage with beurre blanc served with prawns and crab claws.You could call this "comfort cooking", and whilst that wouldn't be inaccurate, it is truer to call it 'Kerry" cooking, for Mr Hallissey's inclination is towards the local and the domestic, rather than to imported ideas and imported ingredients. It is this sense of place that shines through in Packie's: local people working and creating in a legendary local restaurant.You don't just get great food here, you get a great local experience, a true experience founded on generosity. Priceless, so.

- **OPEN:** 6pm-10pm Mon-Sat. Weekends only Nov-Dec. Open one week before Christmas. Closed mid Jan-mid Feb
- **PRICE:** Dinner €45-€50
- **CREDIT CARDS:** Visa, Mastercard, Laser

- **NOTES:**

Wheelchair access, but no disabled toilet.

- **DIRECTIONS:**

In the centre of Kenmare.

10 GREAT

VALUE RESTAURANTS

1
ALEXIS BAR & GRILL
COUNTY DUBLIN

2
L'ATMOSPHERE
COUNTY WATERFORD

3
CHAPTER ONE
COUNTY DUBLIN

4
THE CHART HOUSE
COUNTY KERRY

5
GINGER
NORTHERN IRELAND

6
L'GUEULETON
COUNTY DUBLIN

7
THE MILL RESTAURANT
COUNTY DONEGAL

8
LA MARINE
COUNTY WEXFORD

9
NEPHIN RESTAURANT
COUNTY MAYO

10
TOWN BAR & GRILL
COUNTY DUBLIN

THE BALLYMORE INN

Georgina & Barry O'Sullivan
Ballymore Eustace
County Kildare
+353 (0) 45-864 585
www.ballymoreinn.com
theballymoreinn@eircom.net

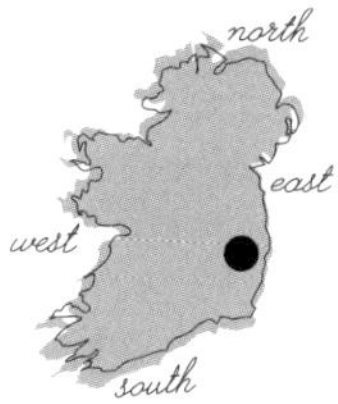

A text-book example of how to create and run a successful restaurant, The Ballymore is one of the great Irish restaurants.

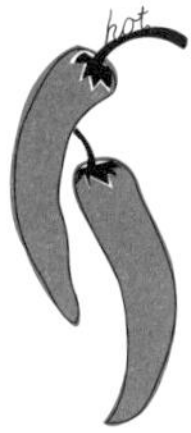

Georgina O'Sullivan is one of the great heroines of Ireland's food culture, someone to rank up there with Myrtle Allen or Maura Foley, someone whose contribution has been as significant intellectually as it has been in a practical way. Her hugely important work with An Bord Bia has been followed by the creation of a restaurant that is one of the glories of Ireland's modern food culture, a restaurant that states the uniqueness of the Irish food culture, and which exploits all of its strengths. Throughout all of her menus you can see the most vivid culinary intellect at work, refining ideas, polishing pairings, extrapolating and interpreting, defining and artifying. The result is just some of the most delicious food you can eat, in one of the most elegant and singular of rooms: Slaney lamb with spinach; Margaret's organic chicken with broccoli and ginger salad; sirloin with watercress and horseradish; goat's cheese, roasted pepper and pinenut tart. The pizzas may be the best in the country, the bar food is outstanding, and The Ballymore is as good as it gets.

- **OPEN:** 12.30pm-9pm Mon-Sun
- **PRICE:** Lunch €25, Dinner €45
- **CREDIT CARDS:** All major cards accepted.

NOTES:

Wheelchair access.
Express lunch, €13 for two courses.

DIRECTIONS:

In the centre of Ballymore Eustace, on the right-hand side of the road when coming from Blessington.

THE MILL AT LYONS

Fred Cordonnier
The Village at Lyons
Newcastle, County Kildare
+353 (0) 1-627 0007
www.villageatlyons.com
info@villageatlyons.com

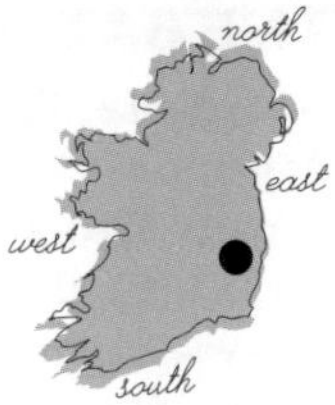

With that fine chef, Fred Cordonnier, now heading up the kitchens, expect more consistency and more culinary chutzpah from The Mill and La Serre.

What a fine thing it was that, at the end of his long and eventful life, Tony Ryan should have decided to build a couple of restaurants, here at the Lyons estate. Flying people around the world is important, we guess, but not half so important as feeding them well, and that is what you will get at the Italian-influenced La Serre, and at the glamorous, luxurious The Mill. Recently, Fred Cordonnier took up the stoves at The Mill, where superstar Richard Corrigan is the public face. M. Cordonnier was cooking mighty food in the Tea Room, in The Clarence Hotel in Dublin, and here his style is radiating energy and culinary clarity. Their signature dishes of Dublin Bay prawns pastilla with caviar are pricey, but you're worth it. Elsewhere an aristocratic restraint decorates the dishes: duo of veal sweetbreads with beetroot rémoulade; poached black sole with morels and truffle gnocchi; turbot with colcannon; pigeon with mead and almond jus; lamb fillet boulangère with dauphinoise potatoes. The food is rich, but light, the hit on the wallet is not light but rich, service is of benchmark standards.

- **OPEN:** noon-2pm Thu-Sun, 7pm-9.30pm Wed-Sat
- **PRICE:** Lunch from €35, Dinner from €80
- **CREDIT CARDS:** All major cards accepted

NOTES:
Full wheelchair access.
Children welcome, especially Sunday lunch

DIRECTIONS:
From the N7 take the road to Newcastle and you will see the signs. Detailed maps are on their website.

BASSETT'S AT WOODSTOCK

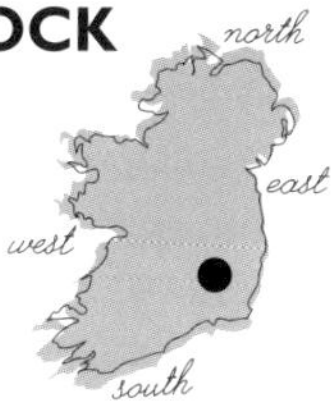

Mijke Jansen & John Bassett
Woodstock Gardens, Inistioge
County Kilkenny
+353 (0) 56-775 8820
www.bassetts.ie
info@bassetts.ie

One of the fave restaurants of the Bridgestone editors, Bassett's is a true star. Stay locally, and make the most of an event.

If you were to take a straw poll amongst the Bridgestone editors, asking them to nominate their absolute fave places to eat throughout the country, Bassett's would be right up there at the top. It's that kind of place. Classy, quirky, individual, unclichéd, run by nice people who love creating nice things for other people to eat and enjoy. "I think the kind of people who use the 100 Best would totally get this place", says Eamon Barrett. What's to get? An idyllic location within the Woodstock demesne that tends to cause the gushing of purple prose when you recall the evening. Inspired cooking that has no precise comparison with anywhere else, which is why hip Bridgestone users will get it: seared tuna with calamari and broad beans; ravioli with sweetcorn and vanilla cream; their own rare breed pork. "Had a most wonderful meal in Bassetts last week, the best ever", writes Claire Goodwillie. "Bassett's - getting better and better. What they do just jumps out at you", writes Eamon Barrett. Bassett's gets better and better. Ask their advice about where to stay, and go for it.

- **OPEN:** noon-4pm, 7.30pm-9.30pm Wed-Sat, noon-5pm Sun
- **PRICE:** Lunch €25, Dinner à la carte, €50, sampling menu €9.50 per dish, nine dishes available
- **CREDIT CARDS:** Visa, Mastercard

NOTES:

Wheelchair access. Dinner: À la carte Wed-Thur, Sampling Sat.

DIRECTIONS:

Follow signs for Woodstock Estate.

ZUNI

Paul & Paula Byrne
26 Patrick Street
Kilkenny, County Kilkenny
+353 (0) 56-772 3999
www.zuni.ie
info@zuni.ie

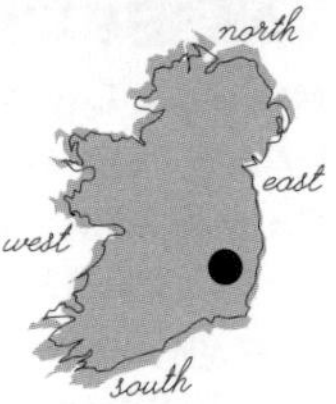

Few rooms can match the electrifying energy of Zuni at its very best: this is a metropolitan experience in Ireland's most Italianate, funky city.

It is Saturday night in Kilkenny, the opening night of the first Savour Kilkenny Festival, and the energy in the dining room of Zuni is only electric. A hip, happening, stylish crowd, dressed in their best, are setting in to Maria Rafferty's tasting menu – warm goat's cheese with pear dressing; lobster cocktail; blue marlin in seaweed with tempura batter; crab and monkfish laksa; cucumber, chilli and pineapple ice; venison fillet with sundried tomato risotto; confit rabbit leg with lime and coriander dressing; Angus fillet with colcannon cake; chocolate and orange soufflé. Classy modern food, served with wonderful wines from superb Irish independent wine merchants. This is the sort of thing Zuni does superbly: carefully chosen foods and wines, carefully cooked, a glam room, a great night. The restaurant is facing increasingly stiff competition in town these days, notably from the fine cooking in a hip room in Café Sol, and we would love to see more local foods used in the menus, but the experience of this room is still one of the most potent metropolitan culinary experiences you can enjoy anywhere in Ireland.

- **OPEN:** 12.30pm-2.30pm, 6pm-9.30pm Mon-Sat; 1pm-2.45pm, 6pm-8.30pm Sun
- **PRICE:** Dinner €40-€45, Lunch €26
- **CREDIT CARDS:** All major cards accepted.

NOTES:

Wheelchair access.
Early Bird dinner, Sun-Fri, €22.50-€27.50

DIRECTIONS:

110 metres up Patrick Street from the main traffic junction at the road up to the Castle.

THE OARSMAN

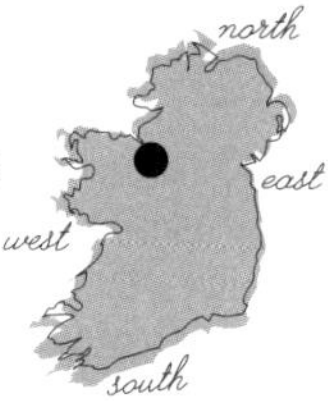

Ronan & Conor Maher
Bridge Street, Carrick-on-Shannon
County Leitrim
+353 (0) 71-962 1733
www.theoarsman.com
info@theoarsman.com

The stars of County Leitrim, Ronan and Conor's rock-solid Oarsman serves great modern cooking in a most beautiful bar and restaurant.

Like their parents before them, Conor and Ronan Maher are not simply masters of hospitality, and purveyors of seriously good food. They are also alephs – points of visualisation – for the sweet little town of Carrick-on-Shannon. It is guys like these who make a town what it is. They work with local producers and use their ingredients superbly. When a journalist from *The Guardian* was writing about Food on the Shannon, the boys could turn to the Leitrim Organic Farmers and the Organic Centre "and so we cooked the lamb off with some local organic veg – baby spinach bursting with flavour – and Tom Maher's rosemary with wild mint mash and it all went down very well". We bet, and now you know where you will get the best cooking on the Shannon. At weekends, food is served in the little back bar as well as upstairs, smart food teamed with great wines: Tom Beirne's pork with spaghetti of carrot and courgette; Paddy Sheridan's lamb with pea and mint mash; darne of salmon wrapped in braised leeks; warm chocolate fondant with pistachio ice cream. Ace food, and an ace place.

● **OPEN:** noon-3.30pm Mon-Wed; noon-2.30pm Thurs-Sat; Dinner served 6.45pm-9.45pm Thurs-Sat.
● **PRICE:** Lunch €17-€20, Dinner €35-€45
● **CREDIT CARDS:** Mastercard/Visa

● **NOTES:**
No children in the bar after 9pm (10pm in summer). wheelchair access in garden room, no disabled toilet.

● **DIRECTIONS:**
In the centre of Carrick-on-Shannon on Bridge St, 100 metres from the bridge.

MARKET SQUARE BRASSERIE

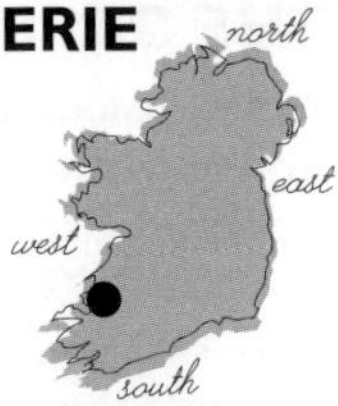

Diarmuid O'Callaghan
74 O'Connell Street
Limerick
County Limerick
+353 (0) 61-316311

Diarmuid O'Callaghan is one of Limerick's most exciting chefs, and he's doing good things in MS.

"Go for Diarmuid O'Callaghan's daily specials" advises Valerie O'Connor, and then you see the very best cooking from this talented chef in a happening cellar room in Limerick city. The room is intimate, classy, with waiting staff in suits and happy troupes of customers, even on a quiet Limerick Tuesday evening, when the place is hoppin'. Kick off with the terrine of foie gras with toasted brioche, and the Liscannor crab cakes, and the night is hot off the blocks: great tastes and textures, punchy, earthy food. Fillet steak with bearnaise and compote of red onion is cooked and served just right, the richness cut by the red onion. John dory with a curried cauliflower purée and vanilla cream sauce is a knockout to look at and even more intriguing to eat, thanks to the presence of blueberries in the sauce, adding richness and sweetness. And after dessert of sticky toffee pudding, Valerie was ready to turn to her Creator and say "OK I'm done, it was great, take me now". Boy, now that is cooking. Steamed apple cake was almost as good. Mr O'Callaghan is doing the good thing in Market Square.

- **OPEN:** from 6pm Tue-Sat
- **PRICE:** Dinner €40
- **CREDIT CARDS:** All major cards accepted

NOTES:
Wheelchair access.
Two sittings, 7pm & 9pm at weekends

DIRECTIONS:
In the centre of Limerick.

THE SAGE CAFÉ

Mike & Siobhan Hogan
67-68 Catherine Street
Limerick, County Limerick
+ 353 (0) 61-409458
www.thesagecafe.com
info@thesagecafe.com

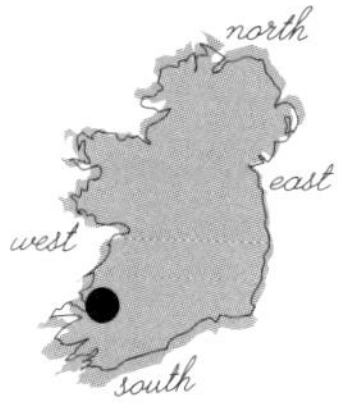

Not just a café, more a local phenomenon, Sage is a starburst of brilliance in Limerick's food culture.

The Limerick Leader, that's Mike and Siobhan's Sage Café. This place has been, as they say locally, "out the door" ever since they opened. "A food phenomenon... a roaring success" is how Valerie O'Connor describes it, and how fine and dandy for Limerick to have a food phenomenon.

So, what's phenomenal? First off, don't get there late, or you won't get a table, and remember you can't book. Second, when you do get a table, settle in for some sharp cooking: artichoke risotto with sweet potato and pancetta; lamb's liver with mustard crushed potatoes, rosemary and lentil jus and crispy red onions; their fine beef hot-pot with baby beetroot and mushrooms; hearty braised lamb shank with cannellini bean and potato stew. This is rich, rustic, savoury food, and they don't put a foot wrong, certainly not when it comes to a baked orange cheesecake that is, says Valerie, "the best baked cheesecake I've eaten". Sage is successful, admirable, and absolutely spot on, with great staff who are right into the buzz of the place. Ace.

- **OPEN:** 9am-6pm Mon-Sat
- **PRICE:** Main courses around €12
- **CREDIT CARDS:** Visa, Mastercard, Laser

NOTES:

Hot food stops at 4pm. Wine menu.
Wheelchair access.

DIRECTIONS:

Parallel to O'Connell Street in the centre of Limerick.

THE WILD GEESE

David Foley & Julie Randles
Rose Cottage, Main Street
Adare, County Limerick
+353 (0) 61-396451
www.thewild-geese.com
wildgeese@indigo.ie

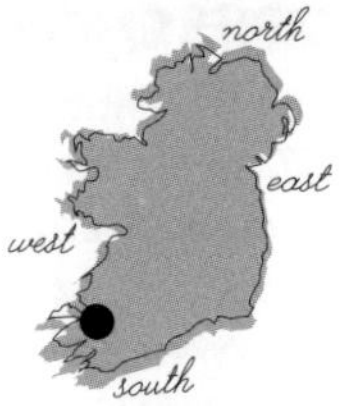

The prettiest restaurant, in the prettiest town, is also one of Ireland's most professional, reliable restaurants.

They are so comfortable in their skins, are David Foley and Julie Randles, that it's no surprise that they should, together, run such an outstanding restaurant as The Wild Geese. He cooks, she runs the restaurant, but it is the power of their combined talents that makes this such a special place: they make the magic together, no less, in terms of culinary aesthetics, hospitality aesthetics, whatever aesthetics you care to name.

Mr Foley's cooking is comforting and cutting-edge, which may sound like a contradiction in terms, but it is something he pulls off with ease. He likes to put two contrasting main elements in a dish – monkfish topped with crabmeat; breast of barbary duck with a spring roll of duck leg confit – and then he uses vegetables and starches to counterpoint these, serving crushed potato, basil, tomato and tapenade with the monkfish, and savoy cabbage with a red wine jus with the duck. It makes for eating where the senses are always being stimulated, re-charged, invigorated; beautiful food that is a joy to eat. Ms Randles, meantime, is simply one of the finest hosts.

- **OPEN:** 6.30pm-10pm Tue-Sun (closed Sun off season)
- **PRICE:** Dinner €40
- **CREDIT CARDS:** Visa, Mastercard, Laser, Amex

- **NOTES:**

Wheelchair access but no disabled toilet. Early bird Tue-Fri, 6.30pm-7.30pm, €30

- **DIRECTIONS:**

On the Main Street of Adare village, near the gates of Adare Manor and just opposite the Dunraven Arms.

ROSSO

Louisa Gilhooly
5 Roden Place, Dundalk
County Louth
+353 (0) 42-935 6502
www.rossorestaurant.com
enquiries@rossorestaurant.com

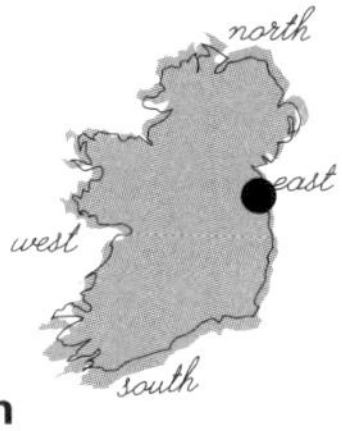

Dundalk has gotten lucky with the arrival of the more-than-fine Rosso, a great destination for Conor Mee's lovely food, and excellent service.

Chef Conor Mee and f-o-h Louisa Gilhooly are doing the good thing in Rosso. Dishes such as roast hake with green beans, smoked ham and grain mustard linguini demonstrate the sort of complex, classy, direct cooking this crew like to send out: outstandingly fine fish, the counterpoint of texture with both the green beans and the mustard linguini, then the deep embrace of the smoked ham to draw all the elements together. Lovely, lovely cooking, cooking that is right on the money and that hits all the marks.

The confidence shown in a single dish such as this is everywhere, and they can even pull off something controversial, like adding some perfectly cooked loin of tuna to a Caesar salad – and make it work. Above all, it is the cleanness of the tastes and textures Mr Mee produces that are so impressive: crab, salmon and shrimp cocktail; duck pastillas with cucumber and soya; slow roast pork fillet with bramley apple and sage; sirloin with slow cooked onions and potato gratin; monkfish and fries with pea purée. Lovely room, fine service, lucky Dundalk.

- **OPEN:** 12.15pm-2.30pm, 6pm-9.30pm Tue-Fri, 6pm-9.30pm Sat, 12.30pm-7pm Sun
- **PRICE:** Lunch €12.50, Dinner €40
- **CREDIT CARDS:** Visa, Mastercard, Laser

NOTES:
No wheelchair access. Pre-theatre dinners to co-incide with local productions.

DIRECTIONS:
Directly opposite St Patrick's Cathedral.

NEPHIN RESTAURANT, MULRANNY

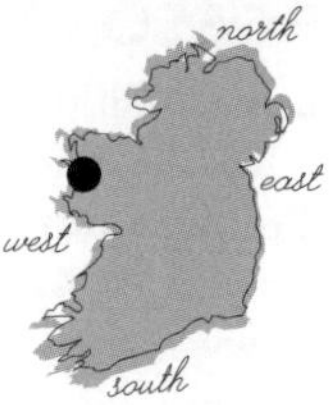

Seamus Commons
Park Inn Mulranny
Mulranny, Westport, County Mayo
+353 (0) 98-36000
www.mulranny.parkinn.ie

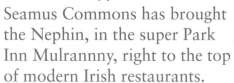

Seamus Commons has brought the Nephin, in the super Park Inn Mulrannny, right to the top of modern Irish restaurants.

We never doubted that Seamus Commons would make the Nephin into one of the best places to eat in Ireland, but we didn't think that he would have achieved it as quickly as his third season. But, a late August stay over in a rollickingly busy hotel proved that Mr Commons is right up there with the very best in Ireland, producing food that is original, spectacular, signed with a vivid signature that is this man's alone. The dishes read complicated – roast rump of lamb, artichoke purée, tomato and mint chutney, pomme fondant, fennel, mustard seed and vintage port cream is a typically wordy main course – but a mixture of skill and vision help Mr Commons bring every tasty morsel home safely. That vision is important: this is amongst the most painterly cooking in Ireland, with vivid swathes of colour and form enshrined on every plate, from dazzling starters such as smoked cheese and pineapple tartlet, via delicious mains of monkfish with asparagus and summer truffle pannacotta through to sublime, fresh, light desserts. Value for money for such food is extraordinary.

- **OPEN:** 7pm-9pm Mon-Sun
- **PRICE:** Dinner €49 (5-course table d'hote menu)
- **CREDIT CARDS:** Visa, Mastercard, Laser

- **NOTES:**

Full wheelchair access. Breakfast served in restaurant, 8am-10.30am, Bar lunch served 12.30pm-9pm, approx €11 for main course.

- **DIRECTIONS:**

On the N59 just outside Newport and overlooking the sea at Mulranny.

THE RESTAURANT AT NUREMORE

Julie Gilhooly, Nuremore Hotel
Carrickmacross, County Monaghan
+353 (0) 42-966 1438
www.nuremore.com
info@nuremore.com

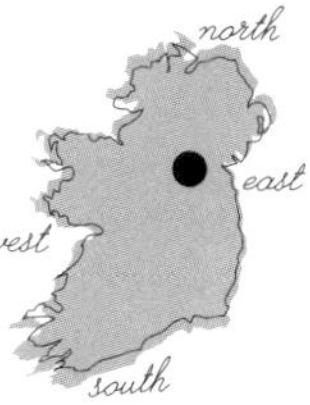

A restless, self-critical team, who are always looking to improve their offer, explains the enduring success of the Nuremore in all its myriad ways.

They don't rest at The Nuremore, and if you knew owner Julie Gilhooly and chef Raymond McArdle, that wouldn't surprise you one bit. They are restless people, always looking to tweak, improve, make better, make new, to show their latest influences and styles, inspirations and the fruits of their travelling and eating. It explains why this hotel and golf complex has such an energy, why its staff seem so committed, why they do things so well – we were guests at a wedding here, one time, and the cooking for a humungous number of guests was truly superb. That sort of application explains why the Nuremore is, for example, full every Xmas, and it explains its enduring appeal and success.
So, they are working on the rooms, and they are simplifying the dining room. As he gets a little older, Ray McArdle is simplifying the rich cooking that has made his name, making sure he is in step with – and indeed one step ahead of – an audience who want to eat well, but a little more lightly. The food is beautifully, obsessively accomplished, and make sure to stay two nights at least.

- **OPEN:** 12.30pm-2.30pm, 6.30pm-9.30pm Mon-Sun (no lunch on Sat, closed 9pm Sun)
- **PRICE:** Lunch €25, Dinner €52-€80
- **CREDIT CARDS:** Visa, Mastercard, Amex,

NOTES:
Wheelchair access - ramp from car park, no steps to restaurant.

DIRECTIONS:
1.5km south of Carrickmacross on the principal N2, Dublin-Derry route, signposted at the entrance.

BROCKA ON THE WATER

Anthony & Anne Gernon
Kilgarvan Quay
Ballinderry
County Tipperary
+353 (0) 67-22038

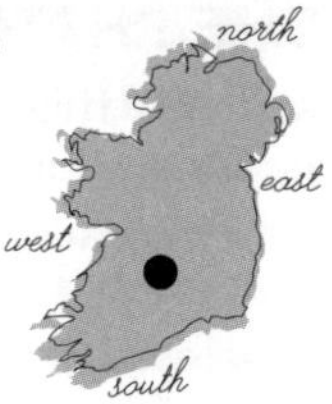

There is no luxury experience quite like the luxury experience of eating at the inimitable, amazing Brocka.

Brocka makes Bridgestone redundant. We can tell you about Anthony and Anne and Nancy's restaurant – and we have been doing so for many years now. And yet, you simply have to come and eat here to understand what Brocka is all about, because Brocka just isn't like anywhere else. Take our mate Sile: worked with us for years – poor dear! – but it was only with a recent, first visit that Sile got it. "Brocka! Amazing! Brilliant! Fantastic!" (Sile's conversation can tend toward hyperbole, with a marked lack of verbs and other conventional conversational devices.) The thing is, Sile's response is pretty standard for those who finally lose their Brocka virginity. For this restaurant within a house, close to the lough, where Nancy and Anne cook and Anthony tends to f-o-h, does things its own way. When we talk about mavericks, then Brocka is what we mean. Their food, their place, their style: amazing!brilliant!fantastic! Hell, who needs verbs.So, permit yourself the magic of this simply unique experience, an experience that defines "luxury" in the most profound, noble, vivid, Irish vernacular way.

- **OPEN:** 7pm-10pm Mon-Sat. Reservations only.
- **PRICE:** Dinner €55
- **CREDIT CARDS:** No credit cards

NOTES:
Wheelchair access. Booking essential off season.

DIRECTIONS:
On Kilgarvan Quay on the Lough Derg Drive, half way between Nenagh and Portumna. From the N52, turn at Borrisokane for Ballinderry.

CHEZ HANS & CAFÉ HANS

Jason Matthiae,
Stefan & Hansi Matthiae
Moor Lane, Cashel, County Tipperary
● Chez Hans +353 (0) 62-61177
● Café Hans & +353 (0) 62-63660

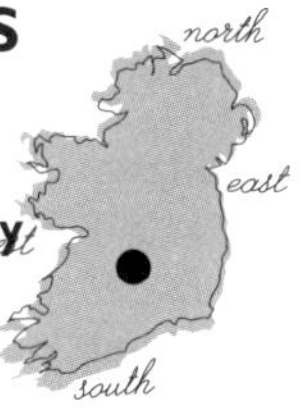

Forty years of outstanding cooking in Chez Hans is something the entire country should celebrate this year.

All hail the birthday boy! In 2008 Chez Hans will be a youthful 40 years old, with the young sibling, Café Hans, a mere baby at just three or four years old.
What an achievement! For Hans Peter and his sons, Jason in Chez and Stefan and Hansi in Café, their culinary gifts have bestowed on the people of Tipperary – and the people of Ireland – cooking of surpassing pleasure and delight. Dishes that go right back to 1968 are cooked today in Chez Hans as if they were newly minted: Wexford lobster grilled with lime, chilli and parsley butter; rack of Tipperary lamb with lamb jus; selection of seafood with a cassoulet of beans and a chive velouté, all beautifully achieved, cooked with exactitude, and served with grace in one of the very best dining rooms. In the Café, meantime, the cooking may be simpler, but it is no less heartfelt: Rossmore mussels with herb crumb; the classic coronation chicken salad; gnocchi with pancetta and ricotta; baked prune cheesecake, served with grace in one of the very busiest dining rooms. Happy birthday, Hans. Forty more years, please.

● **OPEN:** 6pm-10pm Tue-Sat (Chez Hans); noon-5.30pm Tue-Sat (Café Hans)
● **PRICE:** Lunch (Café) €20, Dinner (Chez) €55-€60
● **CREDIT CARDS:** Visa, Mastercard, Laser (Chez Hans). No credit cards accepted in Café Hans.

● **NOTES:**
Wheelchair access. No bookings taken in Café Hans. Early Bird menu 6pm-7.15pm, €28.50-€35 in Chez Hans Tue-Fri.

● **DIRECTIONS:**
Just beside the Rock of Cashel.

LILY MAI'S

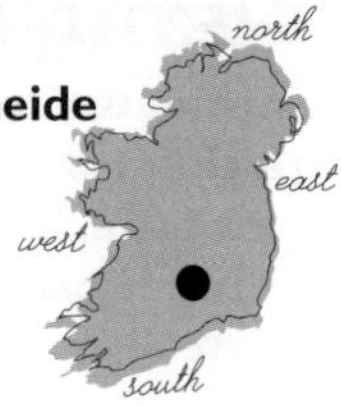

Frances Fogarty & Feargal O Cinneide
Thomastown, Golden, Cashel
County Tipperary
+353 (0) 62-72847
www.lilymais.com
fran@lilymais.com

Confident, classy and capable, Lily Mai's goes about its business with modest excellence, guaranteeing everyone a great dining experience.

With a new food venture at the Dove Hill Centre, just outside Carrick-on-Suir, Frances and Feargal are spreading their mighty talents beyond little Golden.
But, back at base, things continue as well as before in Lily Mai's, with a room that mixes comfort with chic, and with rock-steady cooking, as a recent dinner vividly demonstrated.
Strips of beef with caramelised beetroot and potato cake was spot on, earthy and rich tasting, provocative to the palate, as was a main course of rare fillet of beef with boxty potato, the meat a superb example of local beef cooked to perfection. Dunmore East cod comes with some tiger prawns, which it scarcely needed, and vegetables are fine buttery carrots and sauté potatoes. With desserts, the meal scored the real high points, both sticky toffee pudding and apple and blueberry crumble hitting the sweet spot with ease. Staff are truly excellent, and happily persist with the enlightened tradition of offering one a complimentary glass of Nicholas Feuillette bubbly to begin the evening. Resolutely rock-steady.

- **OPEN:** 6pm-10pm Thu-Sat
- **PRICE:** Dinner €58
- **CREDIT CARDS:** Visa, Mastercard, Laser

- **NOTES:**

Wheelchair access. Reservation highly recommended. The restaurant has a policy of not turning tables.

- **DIRECTIONS:**

In Thomastown village, which is on the main Cashel to Tipperary road.

THE OLD CONVENT

Dermot & Christine Gannon
Clogheen
County Tipperary
+353 (0) 52-65565
www.theoldconvent.ie
info@theoldconvent.ie

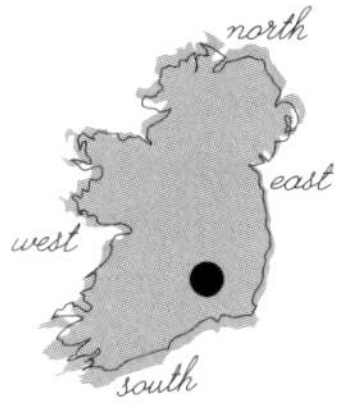

A stylish and unselfconscious shrine to the best Irish cooking, Dermot and Christine's The Old Convent is a mighty star.

"A kitchen operating in the very top echelons" is how Eamon Barrett described the culinary efforts of the crew at TOC. Mr Barrett had been waiting aeons just to get a table for dinner – getting a room borders on the impossible if you only give short notice – but the long-awaited opportunity, thanks to a cancellation, didn't disappoint. Dermot and Christine Gannon have an operation that somehow manages to deliver "comfort food and cutting edge" as Mr Barrett explains it, and the roll-call of dishes on the tasting menu just offers one mind-blowing taste concoction after another: Dunmore East crab blini; Connemara dried lamb with mozzarella; sweet potato velouté with almond butter; lobster and greeen pea mac'n'cheese; lemon and ginger sorbet; 20-hour beef rib with confit potatoes and chanterelle mushroom fricassee; strawberry mint ice cream martini, and finally The Old Convent signature choolate fondue. Perfection in every plate, and a restaurant that is offering not just one of the great Irish experiences, but one of the great European experences.

- **OPEN:** 7.30pm Thu & Sun, 8pm Fri & Sat
- **PRICE:** 8-course tasting menu, €60
- **CREDIT CARDS:** Visa, Master, Laser

- **NOTES:**

No wheelchair access. Children over 12 years welcome.

- **DIRECTIONS:**

The Old Convent is located on the R668 Cahir to Lismore road. A detailed map is available from their website.

L'ATMOSPHERE

Arnaud & Patrice Mary
19 Henrietta Street, Waterford
County Waterford
+353 (0) 51-858426
www.restaurant-latmosphere.com
Latmosphererestaurant@hotmail.com

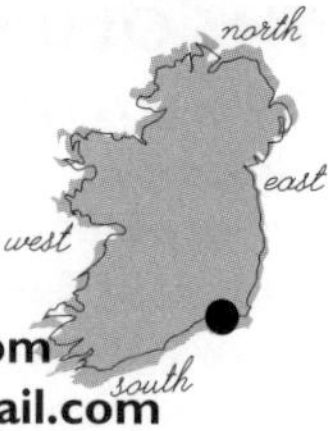

You would pay handsomely for the culinary expertise on offer in L'Atmosphere. Happily, you don't have to, for value for money is superb.

"Rock-solid cooking, real flavours, amazing value." That's how Eamon Barrett summarises the strengths of Arnaud and Patrice Mary's restaurant, and it's hard to think how one could build on a better foundation than that trio of accolades. The rock-solid cooking and real flavours shine through in a dish like slow-roasted lamb, served to the table in its own Le Creuset pot, with lovely slices of lamb, potatoes, green beans and oodles of flavours working everywhichway.

But then another visit will yield up dinner of pan-fried foie gras with cocoa beans and duck jus; fabulous rare tuna (amazingly presented with a little jug of sesame sauce, tall bread and lovely peas with a mother of pearl spoon!); a whole lobster perfectly cooked, and pigeon breast with the rest of the pigeon meat minced and served underneath the breast on a Grand Marnier-soaked piece of toasted bread. Amazing flavours. A chocolate fondant, some vanilla ice cream, perhaps a Temptation Plate - a bit of everything. Fantastic cooking which is beautifully realised, and a star of the south east.

- **OPEN:** 12.30pm-3pm, 5pm-9pm Mon-Fri, 5pm-9pm Sat & Sun
- **PRICE:** Lunch €12.50 main dish, Dinner €35
- **CREDIT CARDS:** Visa, Master, Laser

NOTES:

Wheelchair access. Early bird menu served 5pm-7pm Mon-Sun, €20, includes a glass of wine.

DIRECTIONS:

The narrow Henrietta St. runs off the waterfront close to the Reginald's Tower end of the main quay.

RICHMOND HOUSE

Paul & Claire Deevy
Cappoquin
County Waterford
+353 (0) 58-54278
www.richmondhouse.net
info@richmondhouse.net

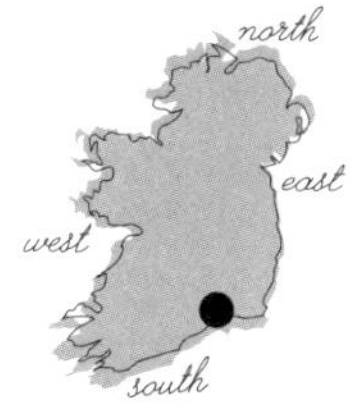

Paul Deevy's cooking eschews showy complexity in favour of delivering sublime tastes and lush textures.

In his wise way, Eamon Barrett once pointed out, regarding Paul Deevy's cooking in the sublime Richmond House, that "Just because cooking may not be complex does not mean that it cannot be accomplished".
Too right! The world is full of chefs who think complexity equals accomplishment, but they are dead wrong. And Mr Deevy, meantime, is dead right, and his country house cooking is as fine an essay of direct, unpretentious cuisine as you will find in Ireland.
If there is a quality about his food that can be described as a personal signature, it is tenderness. His food has myriad textures, but the textures all yield to a melting tenderness, whether you are having Dunmore East scallops with bacon, or Waterford sirloin, or Key Lime pie, or his perfect tempura of Helvick prawns, or just some of the best mashed potatoes you have ever eaten. It is no surprise that as a cook he like to coat his dishes with contrasting overcoats – tempura for prawn; herb crust for Helvick cod; Parma ham wrapped around monkfish, for then the tenderness is emphasised. Just sheer bliss.

- **OPEN:** 7pm-9pm Mon-Sun (closed Sun off season)
- **PRICE:** Dinner €55
- **CREDIT CARDS:** Visa, Mastercard, Amex

NOTES:

Recommended for vegetarians. Wheelchair access with assistance. Early Bird 6pm-7pm €35. Nine guest rooms.

DIRECTIONS:

Just outside the town of Cappoquin, heading in the direction of Waterford city, and clearly signposted from the main road.

THE TANNERY RESTAURANT

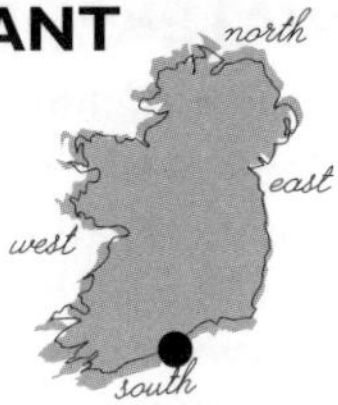

Paul & Máire Flynn
10 Quay Street, Dungarvan
County Waterford
+353 (0) 58-45420
www.tannery.ie
tannery@cablesurf.com

Paul and Maire Flynn's Tannery Restaurant is one of the glories of modern Irish cooking and modern Irish hospitality.

How lucky can you be, to be the kid brought by your folks for Sunday lunch at The Tannery? Roast chicken and mash. Vanilla ice cream and chocolate sauce. Bliss. Would you ever forget those dishes? Would they stay in your mind like Anton Ego's ratatouille in the movie of the same name? When you have kids of your own, would you hope for them to enjoy the same unforgettable tastes, amidst the sublime clamour of kiddie and adult voices that make such a hubbub at The Tannery?
Paul Flynn isn't just a great cook. He is also an educator, someone who opens pleasure portals into the places where only food can take you. He has educated his local audience to appreciate and respect great cooking – beetroot and red onion casserole with Crozier Blue cheese; duck sausage with choucroute and lady apple; pork belly with figs, fennel and Hegarty's cheddar; lasagne of wild rabbit with sage and hazelnut butter – food of its place, in the right place. What Paul and Maire Flynn have achieved in Dungarvan is monumental, and dazzling.

● **OPEN:** 12.30pm-2.15pm Tue-Fri & Sun; 6.30pm-9.30pm Tue-Sat; (6pm-9pm Sun Jul-Aug & bank hols)
● **PRICE:** Lunch €26, Dinner €45-€50, Sun Lunch €30
● **CREDIT CARDS:** Visa, Mastercard, Amex,

● **NOTES:** Wheelchair access. Early Bird dinner, 6.30pm-7.30pm Tue-Fri, €28. The Tannery guesthouse nearby.

● **DIRECTIONS:**
Situated beside the Old Market House building.

WATERFORD CASTLE

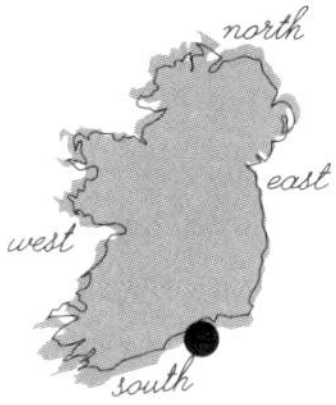

Michael Quinn
Waterford Castle, The Island
Ballinakill, County Waterford
+353 (0) 51-878203
www.waterfordcastle.com
info@waterfordcastle.com

Michael Quinn is one of Ireland's best cooks, and his work in The Castle is a steady, steady upward progress that, happily, shows no sign of stopping.

I'm starting to wonder where the upward trajectory of Michael Quinn's cooking will stop", says Eamon Barrett. "Every visit to the island seems to surpass the previous one, and the restaurant has been embraced by a local crowd". Smart locals, for who wouldn't take the ferry over to taste a tian of Mrs Bates' fresh crabmeat with marinated beetroot with lime crème fraiche and warm brioche? Or smoked duck with duck livers and sherry vinegar glaze? Or buttered Dunmore East lobster with potato rosti, toasted almonds and a lobter cream?
And then settle into main courses such as the plosively tasty O'Flynn's aged beef with sage and truffle polenta cake, or the dynamic meshwork of tastes in Paul Crotty's organic chicken with tagliatelle, girolles, smoked aubergine purée, garlic confit and cep cream? This is fabulous cooking – and the prices represent amazing value for money. With a new management team due to dock in January, the potential for Waterford Castle to build on the triumphant cooking of their star chef is limitless. This cooking simply has to be tasted, has to be.

- **OPEN:** 7pm-8.30pm Mon-Sun
- **PRICE:** Dinner €65 + 10% service charge
- **CREDIT CARDS:** Visa, Mastercard, Amex,

NOTES:
Wheelchair access.

DIRECTIONS:
5 km out of Waterford on the Dunmore East Road. They operate their own ferry to the island.

THE LEFT BANK BISTRO

Annie McNamara & Mary McCullagh
Fry Place, Athlone
County Westmeath
+353 (0) 90-649 4446
www.leftbankbistro.com
info@leftbankbistro.com

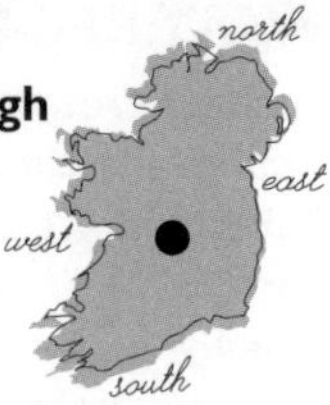

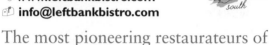

The most pioneering restaurateurs of the Midlands, Annie and Mary continue today to do the good thing in the slinky, left-field Left Bank Bistro.

Ask Annie McNamara how everything is going in the LBB, and she will immediately start telling you how great her staff are, how hard working they are, how long-serving they are, how she is blessed to have them.
Well, says us, and they are blessed to have you.
When you come across a situation like that, you understand how a restaurant like the Left Bank has managed to survive and prosper in a cautious, conservative town like Athlone. When everyone in this neck of the woods wanted steaks, Annie and Mary cooked exciting, light fusion food – turbot with butternut squash and coconut milk purée; cod Mediterranean style with couscous; Asian duck with spiced plum and rosemary; polenta with Fontina cheese and spring vegetables; lamb medallions with black olives and pancetta.
When everyone in this neck of the woods was eating in smoky pubs, Annie and Mary created this glorious, funky, metropolitan room. And today, when folk have money, they continue to offer wonderful value. They are true pioneers, these girls, and their superb staff deserve them.

- **OPEN:** 10.30am-9.30pm (lunch served noon-5pm, dinner served 5.30pm-close) Tue-Sat
- **PRICE:** Main course lunch €12-€14, Dinner €40
- **CREDIT CARDS:** Visa, Mastercard, Amex

NOTES:
Wheelchair access. Early Bird menu 5.30pm-7.30pm Tue-Fri, €25

DIRECTIONS:
On the west side of the Shannon, on the corner of the steep Fry Place.

10 GREAT

CHEFS TO WATCH

RUAIRI DE BLACAM
BIALANN & SEOMRAÍ SÓ INIS MEÁIN

SEAMUS COMMONS
NEPHIN RESTAURANT

FRANCOIS CONRADIE
OVER THE MOON

TOM DOYLE
ELY

GEORGE KEHOE
THE WATERFRONT

BRIAN McCANN
SHU

DYLAN McGRATH
MINT

AINE MAGUIRE
THE WINDING STAIR

DIARMUID O'CALLAGHAN
MARKET SQUARE

CARMEL SOMERS
GOOD THINGS CAFÉ

LA DOLCE VITA

Roberto & Celine Pons
6-7 Trimmer's Lane
Wexford
County Wexford
+353 (0) 53-917 0806

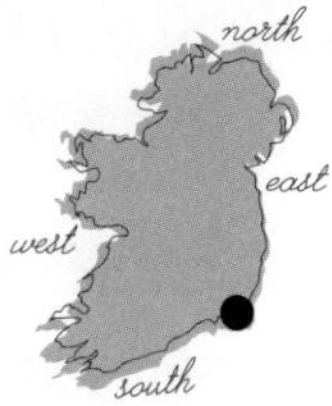

LDV is one of those wonderful restaurants where you will have to queue up and wait for a table, unless you get there very early. Get there early, then.

Was there ever a restaurant so well named as this icon destination in Wexford's Selskar? Roberto and Celine Pons dish out the sweet life every day to their devoted customers, and they do it in the simplest, most logical, most direct way imaginable. Dinners start to arrive around noon, and at about a quarter past the hour, the day's menus are finalised and passed round the punters. By now, chances are there will already be a queue of folk who have missed out on a table.

No matter: they will stand and wait, and try to make you feel guilty as you tear into some gloriously precise and direct Italian cooking: fine antipasti plates mix meats and cooked vegetables and form the perfect shared starter for two people, and then it's some of Italian food's greatest hits, such as tuna e fagioli, or sausage and lentils, or fresh fish with salmoriglio, and then pitch-perfect desserts in the Italian style: tiramisu; pannacotta; orange and lemon tart. Yes, those folk are still waiting, but don't leave without a fine coffee and don't worry about them: this is food worth waiting for, and hunger is the best sauce.

● **OPEN:** 9am-5.30pm Mon-Thur, Fri & Sat 9.30am-10pm
● **PRICE:** Lunch mains €9-€15
● **CREDIT CARDS:** Visa, Mastercard, Laser, Amex

● **NOTES:**
Wheelchair access.

● **DIRECTIONS:**
In the Selskar part of Wexford town.

LA MARINE

Eugene Callaghan
Kelly's Resort Hotel
Rosslare, County Wexford
+353 (0) 53-913 2114
www.kellys.ie

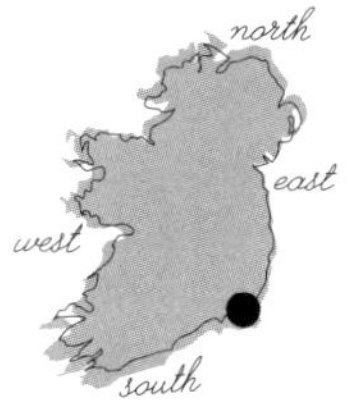

We would like to see the Eugene Callaghan Cookbook published one of these days, a record of great cooking.

There is a great chef's cookery book in Eugene Callaghan, lying there latent amidst all that enviable culinary talent, and someone should facilitate him in writing and publishing it. It wouldn't be the normal sort of chef's book, filled with impossible dishes that need a brigade of chefs. Instead, it would be one of those quiet, slow, philosophical books, like Alice Water's *Chez Panisse Menu Cookbook*, or Koffmann's *Memories of Gascony*, or Bertolli's *Cooking by Hand*.

For that's the kind of cook Mr Callaghan is: slow, philosophical, mining out, in his work, not just the technicalities of cooking, but the very meaning of cooking. This depth gives his cooking astounding savour, whether you are trying the duck confit – absolutely the best there is – with spiced lentils, or the cod with bean and herb broth and garlic aioli, or the pike with beurre blanc, or the pavlova with Wexford berries and chantilly cream. Simple food, yes, but depthless in its import, its understanding, its sense of the intuition which great cooking needs and demands. So, bring on dinner, and the book.

- **OPEN:** 12.30pm-2.15pm, 2.30pm-5pm snack menu, 6.30pm-9.30pm Mon-Sun. Closed mid Dec-late Feb
- **PRICE:** Lunch/snack menu €7-€25, Dinner €34
- **CREDIT CARDS:** Visa, Mastercard, Laser, Amex

NOTES:

Wheelchair access with advance notice. Off season early bird menu, 6.30pm-7.15pm, €21-€26

DIRECTIONS:

Kelly's Hotel is well signposted from in the area. La Marine has a separate entrance.

AVOCA

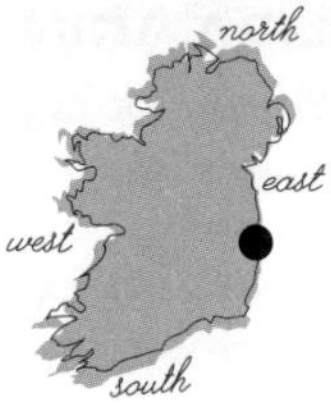

The Pratt family
● Kilmacanogue, Co Wicklow 01-286 7466 ● Suffolk St, D2 01-672 6019 ● Powerscourt, Enniskerry, Co Wicklow 01-204 6070 ● N7 Naas Rd, Rathcoole 01-257 1810 www.avoca.ie

Avoca is Ireland's leading luxury brand, a purveyor of sublime experiences in each and every branch of this mighty, meticulous organisation.

Let's make it official: now that the superb Avoca store and its Egg restaurant and café have opened at Rathcoole, just beside the N7 as you head south, we can officially rename this suburban hamlet. Rathcool. Rathcool it is, thanks to Avoca.

Wherever Avoca goes, it sprinkles magic dust. We have described the Pratt family's organisation as "Ireland's Leading Luxury Brand", and so it is: superb food, superb stores, a superb aesthetic that no one else can match, a class organisation that always outpaces its rivals, by a country mile. And everything is founded on brilliant cooking: last time in Rathcool the McKenna parents and kids ate: Indian chicken curry with rice and salad; beef lasagne with Parmesan and rocket; great chicken and broccoli bake; savoury tart of ricotta and tomato, and everything was perfect, and the sun shone and folk sat on the verandah, and it was all so darn civilising. And then we spent a mess of money downstairs, as you do, as you always do. Rathcool. Luxury Brand. Well, I never...

● **OPEN:** Suffolk St 10am-5pm; Rathcoole 9.30am-5pm Mon-Sat, 10am-5.30pm Sun, Kilmacanogue, Co Wicklow 9.30am-5pm Mon-Fri, 10am-5pm Sat, 10am-5.30pm Sun; Powerscourt 9.30am-5pm Mon-Sat
● **PRICE:** Lunch €20
● **CREDIT CARDS:** Visa, Mastercard, Laser, Amex

● **NOTES:**
Wheelchair access in Kilmacanogue & Rathcoole

● **DIRECTIONS:**
See website for store locations.

GRANGECON CAFÉ

Richard & Jenny Street
Tullow Road, Blessington
County Wicklow
+353 (0) 45-857892
grangeconcafe@eircom.net

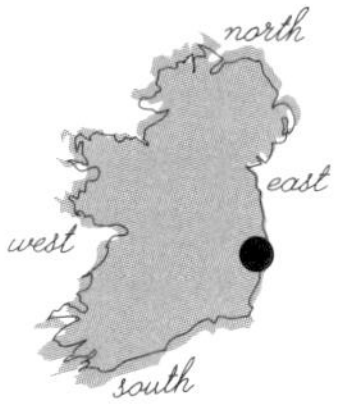

Blessington's iconic destination is as simple a set up as you could imagine, with nothing getting in the way as the mighty, maverick Streets do their stuff.

A local café, serving local foods, with local folk working hard to make sure you enjoy everything, doing things simply, perfectly, working at an inspired level, irrespective of the simplicity of their surroundings. That's what Richard and Jenny serve up in Grangecon, and that's why we love it, and that's why it's in this book. You could serve us that iconic shepherd's pie every day of the week, or the courgette and potato soup, or the red pepper and goat's cheese tart, and then a slice of rhubarb tart, or maybe a piece of chocolate cake, and with a great cup of coffee we would be happy as sandboys. That, after all, is what great food is supposed to be about, that's what great food is all about: simple goodness. Wise Wicklow folk are having a good laugh these days at the arrival of superchefs and 5-star palaces, for who needs that pomp when you have Grangecon? Who needs all that hype when you have this iconic address, a place where goodness itself is what you are served with every slice, every piece, every forkful? What Richard and Jenny do is profound, turning food into philosophy, life into art.

- **OPEN:** 9am-4pm Mon, 9am-5.30pm Tue-Sat
- **PRICE:** Lunch €15-€20
- **CREDIT CARDS:** Visa, Mastercard, Laser

NOTES:

Wheelchair access.

DIRECTIONS:

Blessington is on the N81 route south of Dublin to Enniscorthy. Heading south, turn left at the second set of traffic lights in the village: Grangecon is on the left.

THE STRAWBERRY TREE

Evan Doyle
Macreddin Village, Aughrim
County Wicklow
+353 (0) 402-36444
www.brooklodge.com

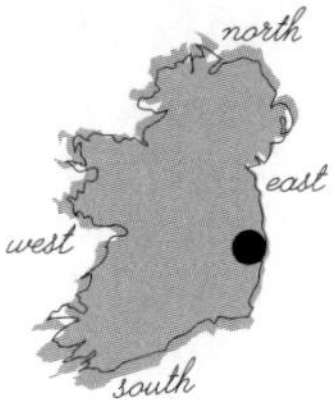

The Feast Menu, served at The Big Table is just the latest inspired idea at Evan Doyle's mighty boutique hotel.

Can we recommend that any groups of people dining in The Strawberry Tree opt for the Feast Menu? This way, what happens is that you sit around the big table and the dishes arrive all at once – home-smoked beef; fabulous seasonal partridge; monkfish in a cream vegetable sauce; rare Wicklow beef; platters of superlative organic vegetables, the dishes roll out until the table is veritably laden with fabulous food. And then you help yourself, and you help each other, and something interesting happens: you realise that what Evan Doyle and his crew have done is to connect you to something primal, the act of sharing that is such an integral part of a group of people eating together. Team work? Bonding? Huh, this is team work on a whole other level.
The Feast Menu at the Big Table is one of the most radical ideas Evan Doyle has had, but radical ideas come quickly to this brilliant organisation, largely because they are expert in tapping into our subconscious with what they offer. The Strawberry Tree gives us what we want, whether we are two, or twenty. Great staff, great place.

- **OPEN:** 7pm-9.30pm Mon-Sat; 1.30pm-3.30pm Sun
- **PRICE:** Lunch €40, Dinner €65
- **CREDIT CARDS:** Visa, Mastercard, Laser, Amex

NOTES:
Wheelchair access. Macreddin Village encompasses the Brook Lodge hotel, a market, shop, pub and Spa.

DIRECTIONS:
From Aughrim follow the signpost to Macreddin Village (3km). They will send detailed directions if requested: good idea!

Northern Ireland

ALDEN'S

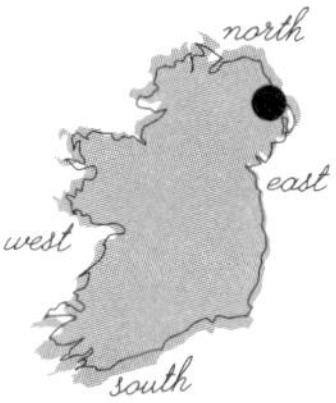

Jonathan Davis
229 Upper Newtownards Road
Belfast, County Antrim
+44 (0) 28-9065 0079
www.aldensrestaurant.com
info@aldensrestaurant.com

A decade of the most competent, unassuming culinary success has been the USP of Belfast's brilliant Alden's.

Good judgment has always been the secret to the success of Jonathan Davis's Alden's resturant, and through the course of ten years – they opened first in 1998 – we have never known that judgement to falter, never mind to even deign to slip.

Service, value, cooking, ambience, inventiveness, and attention to detail were born fully fledged here, and have gone on to a magnificent maturity. They make a perfect Caesar salad – no tandoori chicken here! – and steamed mussels are simply served with scallions, white wine and cream. A twice-baked soufflé of spinach and goat's cheese with chive cream is soufflé heaven, and haunch of rabbit with spring cabbage, pine nuts and raisins, or grilled coquelet with lemon and mint cous cous vie only with each other in the deliciousness stakes.

This is masterly cooking, cooking with elegance, history, pedigree, and modernity, cooking that is a primer of first culinary principles and a statement of culinary individuality. Mr Davis is one of the great restaurateurs, with a decade at the helm of one of the great restaurants.

● **OPEN:** noon-2.30pm Mon-Fri; 6pm-10pm Mon-Sat (till 11pm Fri & Sat)
● **PRICE:** Lunch £7-£13, Dinner £25-£30
● **CREDIT CARDS:** All major cards accepted

● **NOTES:**
Wheelchair access. Special Dinner menu, £18.50-£22.75 Mon-Thu

● **DIRECTIONS:**
On the Upper Newtownards Road, near the cross roads with Sandown Road.

10 GREAT

MAVERICKS

PASCAL BRADLEY
101 TALBOT

PETER CAVISTON
CAVISTON'S

DERMOT & CHRISTINE GANNON
THE OLD CONVENT

ANTHONY & ANNE GERNON
BROCKA-ON-THE-WATER

BEN GORMAN
THE MERMAID

SEAN KEARNEY
O'CALLAGHAN-WALSHE

AOIBHEANN MCNAMARA
ARD BIA

TOM O'CONNELL
O'CONNELL'S

NICK PRICE
NICK'S WAREHOUSE

RICHARD & JENNY STREET
GRANGECON CAFÉ

PAUL ARTHURS

Paul Arthurs
66 Main Street
Kircubbin, County Down
+44 (0) 28-4273 8192
www.paularthurs.com
info@paularthurs.com

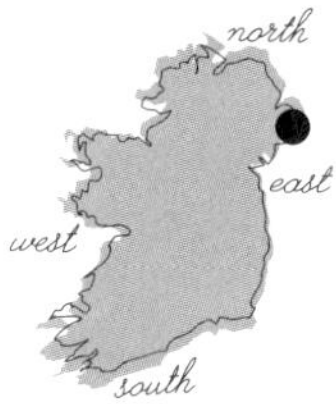

Not every dish reaches the stars in Paul Arthurs, but the misses are forgiven and forgotten when you encounter the sheer brilliance of the food.

"The greatness occludes the weaknesses", says Gillian Bolton. And that's the beauty of Paul Arthurs's eponymous restaurant, to be honest. He is a human cook, a busy guy running a restaurant with rooms and a chipper in little Kircubbin, and so the stresses and unpredictabilities of the professional restaurateur can sometimes end up on your plate – dull tortellini with speck, fontina and shaved Parmesan; soggy bread and butter pudding. Never mind. For every human failing there are dishes for the gods: seared foie gras served on spiced bread with a red wine reduction is sublime; chicken with morels is not just great cooking, but great seasonal cooking, with its rich woodland notes; Finnebrogue venison with champ is faultless; spaghetti with mussels and a saffron cream is glorious. You simply cannot have these glories without some misses, and we would rather have this gifted chef showing all the mercurial magic of the kitchen than being some manner of cooking machine who never misses, but who never hits the stars either. A hands-on human enterprise, then, but one with much greatness.

- **OPEN:** noon-2.30pm, 5pm-9pm Tue-Sat
- **PRICE:** Dinner £30
- **CREDIT CARDS:** Visa, Mastercard, Laser

NOTES:
No Wheelchair access, though there is a stair lift for disabled. Accommodation available, £70 double, £50 single. £10 supplement for children sharing.

DIRECTIONS:
Right in the middle of the main street in the village, on the left-hand side as you drive towards Portaferry.

BALLOO HOUSE

Ronan & Jennie Sweeney
& Danny Millar
1 Comber Road
Killinchy, County Down
+ 44 (0) 28-9754 1210
www.balloohouse.com

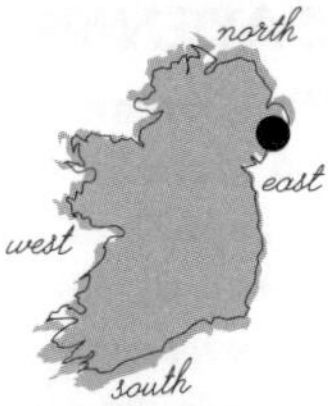

Danny Millar's cooking is so fine you can hardly stop sending text messag-es to tell your friends.

Danny Millar's cooking in Balloo House is right off the radar. "Wow this is gr8 cooking" says Sally's text message after a September dinner. "This is cooking that reminds me of the adventurous pioneering days of irish food. Days when Gerry Galvin would mix oysters with black pudding, Robbie (Millar) would put scallops with avocado. Times when commentators like Andrea Petrini & Emily Green would make a pilgrimage to enjoy the gr8 food going on in Ireland."

Proof of how far Mr Millar can take things is shown in a dish of roast belly of pork with salt 'n' chilli squid, tomato, chorizo, and brandade, all arrayed on the one plate. Can he make it work? Not a bother: this chef can find symmetries of flavour and sympathies of pairing where others would get lost in the hunt. The result is a wow! dish, which is also pretty much the result with everything, especially the superb shellfish cookery. Part of Mr Millar's strength is his intricate knowledge of suppliers: he takes the best, and then he makes the best even better. Balloo is brilliantly, blissfully out of the box.

- **OPEN:** 6pm-9pm Tue-Thu, 6pm-9.30pm Fri & Sat
- **PRICE:** Dinner £25-£35
- **CREDIT CARDS:** All major cards accepted

- **NOTES:**

Bistro food served in the bar noon-9pm Mon-Sun, 'till 8pm Sun. Wheelchair access downstairs only.

- **DIRECTIONS:**

Follow signs for Killinchy and the restaurant is on the roadside.

CAYENNE

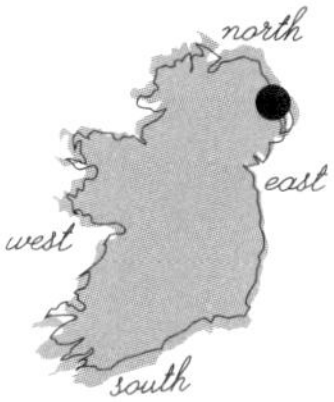

Paul & Jeanne Rankin
7 Ascot House, Shaftesbury Sq,
Belfast, County Antrim
+44 (0) 28-9033 1532
www.rankingroup.co.uk
belinda@rankingroup.co.uk

It may not be at the cutting edge of Belfast cooking any more, but the mighty Cayenne cocktail remains an addictively potent drama of pleasure.

There is still a potency to the Cayenne cocktail of fusion food and funky style, still a strong sense that this landmark restaurant achieves its goals of democratic dining, and high old times. A bunch of suits will be sitting across from you, celebrating getting through another Monday at the office, whilst courting couples swop romantic billet-doux at another table and order up the pricey fizz to celebrate their own personal concoction. The style of the room, once so aggressively post-modernist, has slipped graciously from progressive to retro without ever having to change, proving what a class act it was from the beginning.

The cooking takes no chances, seizing the most elemental and flavourful dishes from the culinary globe – prawn wantons; duck confit; miso soup; steak and chips – and turning them into hand-tooled deliciousness. Desserts, in particular, remain a high point, a blood-sugar blitz of sheer intoxication. Some may regret the fact that Cayenne no longer feels like somewhere at the cutting edge, but its true nature is that it is stand-alone.

- **OPEN:** noon-2.30pm Mon-Fri; 5pm-late Sun-Fri, 6pm-late Sat.
- **PRICE:** Lunch £12-£15.50, Dinner £30-£35
- **CREDIT CARDS:** All major cards accepted

NOTES:

Wheelchair access. Special dinner menu, 5pm-7pm £15.50-£19.50

DIRECTIONS:

At the top of Great Victoria Street in the city centre, Cayenne is easy to find in Shaftesbury Square.

DEANE'S

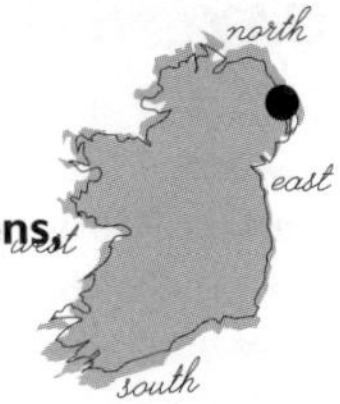

Michael Deane
●Deli, 44 Bedford Street,
+ 44 (0) 28 9024 8800 ●at Queens,
1 College Garden, 9038 2111
●Restaurant Michael Deane, 34
Howard St, 9033 1134
Belfast www.michaeldeane.co.uk

Which of the three Deane's should you choose? Here's the verdict of the Bridgestone jury.

With three separate city restaurants – Deane's; Deane's Deli and Deane's At Queens, Michael Deane presents us with the Paradox of Choice. As with any paradox, choices can prove unpredictable, which is why we choose Deane's Deli as the most exciting of the three. The last meal we had in Deane's Deli was spectacular, and whilst the original restaurant and the handsome room at Queen's were both extremely good, the Deli knocked our proverbial socks off, producing what can only be described as one of the highlights of the year. What separated the experience from the other restaurants was that here the team seemed to be having real fun both with the food and in running the room, a contrast to the unimaginative service elsewhere. And with this relaxed vibe came food that spoke to the gods: walnut-crusted goat's cheese with carrot jam; an awesome special of seafood risotto; classy prawn cocktail; brilliant smoked chicken salad; fantastic Kettyle beef ribeye with mushroom ketchup; great Portavogie haddock and chips, the former with a great Hilden Ale batter. Special.

● **OPEN:** Deli noon-3pm, 5pm-9pm Mon-Tue, noon-3pm, 5pm-10pm Wed-Fri, noon-10pm Sat; Restaurant noon-3pm, 6pm-10pm Mon-Sat; Queen's 11.30am-3pm, 3pm-5pm Mon-Sat, 5pm-9pm Mon-Tue, 5pm-10pm Wed-Sat
● **PRICE:** Deli & Queens Lunch €15-€20, Dinner €25; Restaurant Lunch €16.50-€20.50 Dinner €36
● **CREDIT CARDS:** All major cards accepted

● **NOTES:** Wheelchair access.

● **DIRECTIONS:**
All three restaurants are in the centre of Belfast.

THE DUKE RESTAURANT

Ciaran Gallagher
The Duke Bar
7 Duke Street
Warrenpoint, County Down
+44 (0) 28-4175 2084
www.thedukerestaurant.com

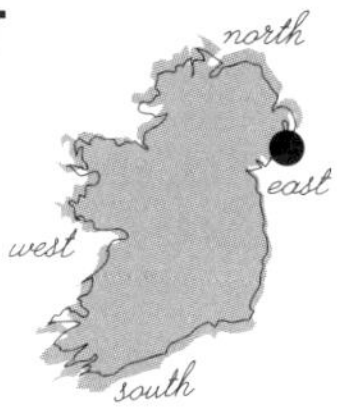

Ciaran Gallagher's restaurant continues to pack in the Warrenpoint punters, day after day, with great cooking, fine service and great value for money.

It doesn't seem to matter just when you turn up to eat at The Duke: the place will be buzzing whether it's a wet Wednesday or a tranquil Sunday early evening, which was when Gillian Bolton and her mate Jillian got a table for dinner. Things got off to a great start: a timbale of diced blue potatoes dressed with vinaigrette, avocado and a mixture of flaked seafood topped with a few fresh salad leaves is delightful, light, fresh if a tad under seasoned. Prawns in a creamy Thai-scented sauce and some sticky rice is just as good, showing how confident Mr Gallagher and his team are in riffing through the global culinary catalogue.
Mains are just as full of tasty aplomb: cooked sliced loin of lamb with a balsamic jus and baby potatoes is ace, whilst haddock "breadcrumbed" with couscous and served with peas and chorizo is imaginative and astutely executed. What a pity that puddings are a weak point; both crème brulée and sticky toffee pudding are off the beat, through good coffee helps one to quickly forgive this surprising blip. Service is excellent in this local hero.

- **OPEN:** 6.30pm-10pm Tue-Sat, 5.30pm-9pm Sun
- **PRICE:** Dinner £22
- **CREDIT CARDS:** All major cards accepted

NOTES:
Wheelchair access to bar only. Bar lunch served noon-2pm Tue-Sat, £34.50. Mid-week special dinner menu £13.95 for three courses.

DIRECTIONS:
From Newry 9.5km on the A2. Just off the square in the centre of Warrenpoint, upstairs over the Duke bar.

GINGER

Simon McCance
68-72 Great Victoria Street
Belfast
County Antrim
+44 (0) 28-9024 4421
www.gingerbistro.com

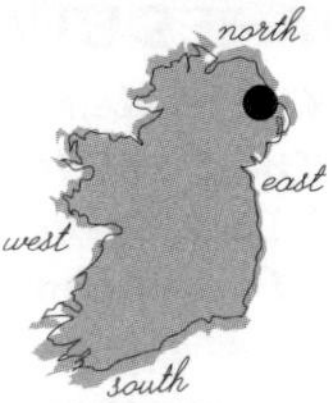

A city-centre restaurant on a mighty roll, Simon McCance and his crew are producing some of Northern Ireland's best cooking, all in their own style.

If you can define style as being the preserve of people who have the nerve to be defiant about a lack of style, then Simon McCance is the Christian Dior of his alternative style universe. Christian Dior? Hell, this guy is John Galliano and Alexander McQueen all in one.

The carelessness about the style of Ginger is so funky, so proud, that you would have to travel to Barcelona to see other rooms that have such insousiance, such freedom from the tyranny of design.

As with the room, so with the food. Mr McCance has always had the most individualistic of culinary signatures, his food seeming to pull in influences but never being subsumed by them: haunch of venison with oyster mushrooms and red wine; parsnip and chickpea fritter; puff pastry pie of spinach and ricotta. He cooks the way Aussie and Spanish guys do, bringing flavours to dishes that then positively sparkle with clean, fresh energy and taste, but presenting the food in such a confident, unclichéd way that the overall content of Ginger – its bohemianism, defiance, originality, its style – become all of a piece.

- **OPEN:** noon-3pm Thu-Sat, 5pm-10pm Tue-Sat
- **PRICE:** Lunch £10-£13, Dinner £28.50
- **CREDIT CARDS:** Visa, Mastercard, Maestro

● NOTES:
Wheelchair access. Pre-theatre menu 5pm-7pm Tue-Fri, £11

● DIRECTIONS:
200m up the street from the Crown Bar, leading out of the city and smack on the main strip of Great Victoria Street.

JAMES STREET SOUTH

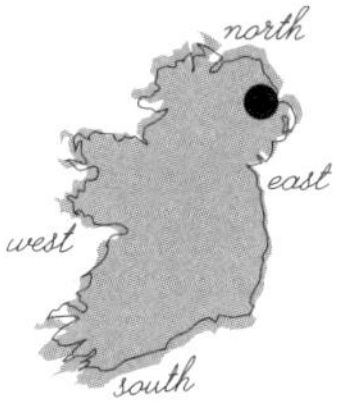

Niall McKenna
21 James Street South
Belfast, County Antrim
+44 (0) 28-9043 4310
www.jamesstreetsouth.co.uk
info@jamesstreetsouth.co.uk

Some of the most accomplished, painterly-perfect cooking is what Niall McKenna produces in the lovely JSS.

He isn't a relation of ours, Niall McKenna – and no, Clodagh McKenna isn't a relative either, since you asked: she's from the polite Armagh McKennas, whilst we are the wild, white-haired bunch from Monaghan – and it's a genuine shame, because this is one cook you wouldn't mind having around to help you with the barbecue. There is such finesse to Mr McKenna's work, such painterly perfection, that with him at the grill you would wind up with the barbie from heaven. But what you get in JSS is food from heaven, marvellously considered, concocted and executed, food that in its assail of tastes and its palette of textures and colours is simply riotous. By nature, he is a purist: dishes have no discordant elements and present themselves correctly – milk-fed veal with white beans and cep cream; lamb with pistachios and apricots, seafood classics like skate with lobster and prawns and beurre noisette – but this is in no way conservative cooking. It's informed by a wide range of influences, but those influences are subsumed rather than made manifest. Sublime.

- **OPEN:** noon-2.45pm, 5.45pm-10.45pm Mon-Sat; 5.30pm-9pm Sun
- **PRICE:** Lunch £13.50-£15.50, Dinner £25-£35
- **CREDIT CARDS:** All major cards accepted

NOTES:
Wheelchair access. Pre-theatre menu £15.50 for two courses, £17.50 for three courses.

DIRECTIONS:
From the City Hall, travel up Bedford Street, and James Street South is the first street on the right.

MOURNE SEAFOOD BAR

Andy Rea
34-35 Bank Street, Belfast
County Antrim
+ 44 (0) 28-9024 8544
www.mourneseafood.com
belfast@mourneseafood.com

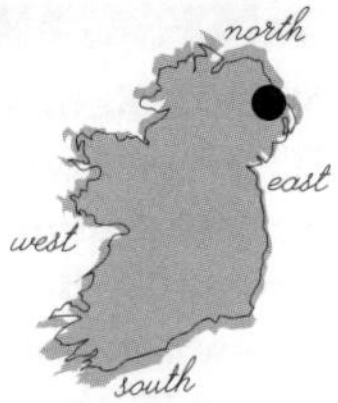

Andy Rea always promised great things, and he has over-delivered on great things in the MSB.

After giving a speech at a food congress near to Belfast which was distinguished by a vivid – a tragic – demonstration of the disenchantment and disillusion of modern Irish farmers, we went to eat at Andy Rea's Mourne Seafood Bar. We had seared scallops with saffron linguini, gremolata and fresh tomatoes, then roast fillet of hake with spinach, new potatoes and a curried mussel cream. The food was so good, so energised, so vital, so clean and crisp, so pure and fresh, that it lifted the gloom of the conference as if in a moment. We just wished that all those melancholy farmers could have been there with us to share food that spoke of sheer goodness, the goodnesss of farms and farmers, of seas and fishermen, of chefs and their kitchens and restaurants.

That's what good cooking can do: it can save your life, it can dispel melancholy – chasse spleen, as the wine has it – it can articulate all the good things in life. Andy Rea is a chef who understands these things, a skilful cook, but an elemental one, first and foremost. Mr Rea gets the point of it all, and so the Mourne is just not to be missed.

- **OPEN:** noon-6pm Sun-Mon, noon-9.30pm Tue-Wed, noon-10.30pm Thur-Sat
- **PRICE:** Lunch £6-£13, Dinner £20-£25
- **CREDIT CARDS:** Visa, Mastercard, Maestro

NOTES:
Wheelchair access.

DIRECTIONS:
Just off Royal Avenue, in between Tesco and Primark.

NICK'S WAREHOUSE

Nick & Kathy Price
35-39 Hill Street
Belfast, County Antrim
+44 (0) 28-9043 9690
www.nickswarehouse.co.uk

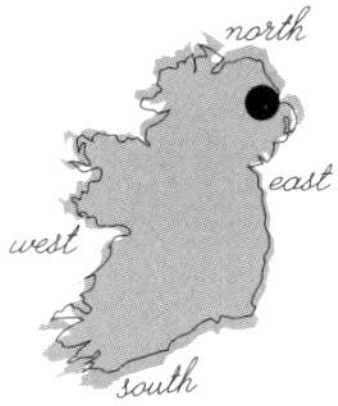

Nick Price's cooking is as wild and freeform as his intellect, and it makes Nick and Kathy Price's restaurant peerless.

There was a bit of a big media to-do in the North when we launched the latest *Bridgestone Irish Food Guide*. Some of this was something to do with Derry, but for the most part it resulted in a big pic of Nick Price, on page 3 of *The Belfast Telegraph*, with a caption underneath declaring "Nick Price: described as the 'single most important cook in the history of Northern Ireland'".
So, is he? He sure is. Only Florence Irwin gets anywhere near to Mr Price as a cook, an educator, a sage, an epicurean, and an all-round-good-thing. His cooking today, after thirty years of rattling the pans, seems to us to be better than ever. He can cook dishes such as short ribs of Kettyle beef braised in Clotworthy Dobbin ale, uniting two of the North's finest artisan products, and he can make the dish something that speaks more about Northern Ireland's food culture than any other working chef. There really isn't a cliché to be found anywhere in his work, probably because he is so intellectually unclichéd. The Myrtle Allen of Northern Ireland, that's Nick.

● **OPEN:** noon-3pm (wine bar) Mon-Fri, noon-2.30pm (restaurant) Tue-Fri; 6pm-9.30pm Tue-Thur; 6pm-10pm Fri-Sat
● **PRICE:** Wine Bar lunch £12, Restaurant lunch £18-£25, Dinner £27
● **CREDIT CARDS:** All major cards accepted.

● **NOTES:**
Wheelchair access. Check web for on-line wine.

● **DIRECTIONS:**
At the rere of St Anne's Cathedral.

10 PLACES

WITH GREAT SERVICE

1
BIALANN & SEOMRAÍ SÓ INIS MEAIN
ARAN ISLANDS

2
CHAPTER ONE
COUNTY DUBLIN

3
THE CHART HOUSE
COUNTY KERRY

4
MacNEAN RESTAURANT
COUNTY CAVAN

5
THE OARSMAN
COUNTY LEITRIM

6
THE OLDE POST INN
COUNTY CAVAN

7
OSCAR'S
COUNTY GALWAY

8
RICHMOND HOUSE
COUNTY WATERFORD

9
THE SAGE CAFÉ
COUNTY WATERFORD

10
THE WILD GEESE
COUNTY LIMERICK

ROSCOFF BRASSERIE

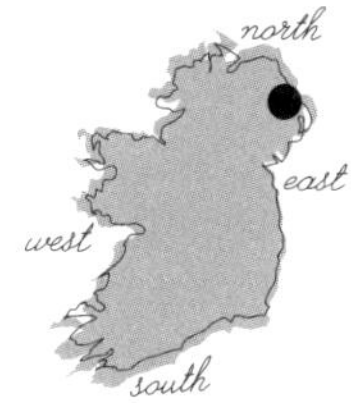

Paul & Jeanne Rankin
7-11 Linenhall Street
Belfast
County Antrim
+44 (0) 28-9031 1150
www.rankingroup.co.uk

As Paul Rankin returns to what he does best, we are relishing the prospect of a Roscoff resurgence: back to the gidddy heights of 1991, please.

It says a lot about Paul Rankin that when he talks to the local media, the interviewer is likely to be their Showbusiness Correspondent. But Mr Rankin's last chat with the showbiz writer was a reflective one, as he mused on his business difficulties, and the challenges in his family life, and said, "I'm not an out-and-out business man. My passion is cooking".

This is good news for Belfast, for Rankin's restaurants have always been talismans of the city's food culture, and with chef Paul Waterworth firing away at the stoves in Roscoff, the time for the Rankin resurgence has begun. The Roscoff Brasserie has been the most consistent and imaginative of the Rankin brand in recent years, and the cooking has been a solid-sender of contemporary French-influenced cuisine, the kind of food with which Rankin made his name. So, with a new focus on "our core values, we are passionate about food and committed to excellence" said Rankin, this crew should have only one objective in mind: to hit once again the giddy culinary and restaurant heights they hit back in 1991.

- **OPEN:** noon-2.15pm Mon-Fri, 6pm-10.15pm Mon-Thur, 6pm-11.15pm Fri & Sat
- **PRICE:** Lunch, £15.25-£19.50, Dinner £24-£33
- **CREDIT CARDS:** All major cards accepted

NOTES:
Wheelchair access. 6pm pre-theatre dinner

DIRECTIONS:
At the rere of the City Hall in central Belfast

SHU

Alan Reid
253 Lisburn Road
Belfast, County Antrim
+44 (0) 28-9038 1655
www.shu-restaurant.com
eat@ shu-restaurant.com

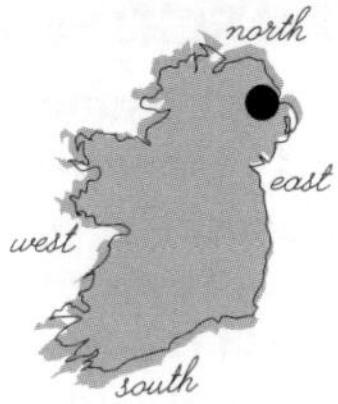

Brian McCann is one of the city's – and the country's – hottest culinary talents, and you simply must taste his cooking.

Brian McCann is the chef's chef in Belfast these days, a rip-roaring culinary talent riding the crest of critical and popular acclaim. And the proof of the sort of dynamic kitchen he is working in was further underlined earlier in the year when Chris McClurg, part of the Shu crew, won the first ever Robbie Millar Scholarship. These guys are happening.

Mr McCann's cooking is as smart as it gets, and whilst the à la carte may be somewhat tamer than when he started, the cooking will blow you away with its intricate yet common-sense pairings and adaptations: that note of 5-spice with Glenarm salmon; lovely chestnut gnocchi with venison; pigeon with fine tart of pear and celeriac; hake beautifully paired with beurre noisette and a clean parsley risotto; sage and onion mash with perfect calves' liver. Everywhere you taste, some logical and delicate grace note has been found to take the ingredients out of the quotidian and into the taste stratosphere, making for some of the best cooking to be found in the country, food that is an essay is sympathy, appreciation and care.

- **OPEN:** noon-2.30pm, 6pm-10pm
- **PRICE:** Lunch £16, Dinner £17.50-£33
- **CREDIT CARDS:** All major credit cards accepted

NOTES:

No wheelchair access. Business lunch and Express menu served at lunchtime.

DIRECTIONS:

Straight up the Lisburn Road, across the road from Windsor Avenue.

THYME

Conor McCann, Austin Finn & Nichola Walls
Blackwood Golf Club
150 Crawfordsburn Road,
Bangor, County Down
+44 (0) 28 9185 3394

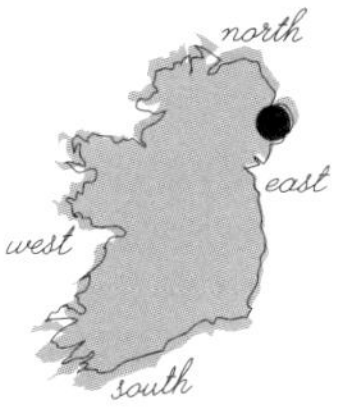

Tentativeness and inexperience are a charming part of the charm of Thyme, a great new food adventure.

Conor McCann, Austin Finn and Nicola Walls, the three players behind Thyme, are inexperienced but sincere, and their enthusiasm is infectious. They are three amongst the new school of ultra-smart, ultra-well-informed restaurateurs in the North, and they are courageous. As they explain on the menu, "The word Thyme is derived from the Greek word Thymon meaning courage".
That isn't a bit fanciful: their courage is an essential part of the magic they are creating here, and whilst the menu may read like many others – pork belly with scallops; dry-aged beef; turbot with ginger and lemongrass; raviolo of quail – there is already a signature style here, and Mr McCann has talent aplenty, as he shows with impeccably cooked dishes such as rack of lamb smoked with garlic with a warm salad of green beans and shallots, or smoked lobster with asparagus and a citrus beurre blanc, or in pitch-perfect foie gras with caramelised orange salad and cumberland sauce. This is fine cooking, and the tentativness of everything in Thyme is rather magical. A new journey begins, on the well-worn, honorable path.

- **OPEN:** noon-3pm, 6pm-10pm Wed-Fri, 'till 11pm Fri, 6pm-11pm Sat, 12.30pm-7pm Sun
- **PRICE:** Lunch £16-£21, Dinner £35
- **CREDIT CARDS:** Visa, Mastercard, Maestro

- **NOTES:**

Grill bar opens noon-10pm Wed-Sat, 12.30pm-7pm Sun. Restaurant table d'hote dinner £22-£25 Wed-Fri.

- **DIRECTIONS:**

Part of the Blackwood Golf course, signposted from the A2 Belfast Bangor road, just past the garden centre.

23

Raymond & Andrea McArdle
23 Church Street,
Warrenpoint
BT34 3HN, County Down
+44 (0) 28-4175 3222
restaurant23@btconnect.com

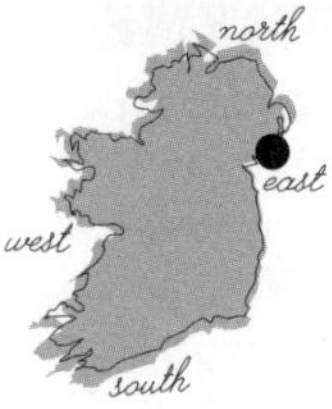

Incredible value for money for marvellous cooking from Trevor Cunningham is the 23 secret. You can bet it won't stay a secret for much longer.

You really do wonder if the good people of Warrenpoint know what a great value gem of a restaurant they have in 23. Sirloin with onion purée and cognac sauce for just over 15 quid! Fillet of Old Spot pork with Calvados sauce for under 15 quid! Folk in Dublin would happily pay three times those prices for Trevor Cunningham's cooking, and they would feel they were getting the best bargain and they would be back two nights out of every week. Such is life in modern Ireland.

So, the simple fact is that Mr Cunningham is firing out amazing food, and is doing so at amazing value for money. It's the kind of classic-yet-modern food that Ray and Andrea McArdle make such a signature of in their restaurants – seabass with tomato and pancetta minestrone; duck wontons with mango mayonnaise; foie gras terrine with quince purée. Care is taken with the smallest details – a brunoise of Mediterranean vegetables stuffed into a plum tomato; fantastic mustard mash; a side salad that tastes so fresh you reckon they must have walked into the garden to pick it. Really ace cooking.

- **OPEN:** 12.15pm-3pm, 6.30pm-10pm Wed-Sat, 12.30pm-8pm Sun
- **PRICE:** Lunch £8-£10, Dinner £20-£30
- **CREDIT CARDS:** All major cards accepted

NOTES:
Wheelchair access.

DIRECTIONS:
From Newry, go straight through the first roundabout in Warrenpoint, take next left within Bennett's bar.

Index

S

T

V

W

Z

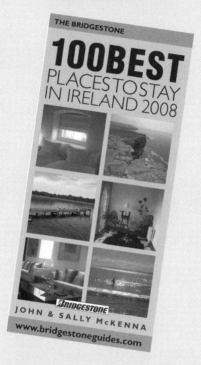

CONTACT THE BRIDGESTONE GUIDES:

We greatly appreciate receiving reports, e-mails and criticisms from readers, and would like to thank those who have written in the past, whose opinions are of enormous assistance to us when considering which 100 restaurants finally make it into this book.

Please write to:

Estragon Press, Durrus, County Cork

Or send an email via:

www.bridgestoneguides.com

www.bridgestoneguides.com

for up-to-date information on all that is happening in Irish food.

The website includes a comprehensive listing of all the great shops, foods, markets and drinks in Ireland, as well as places to stay and eat.

There is also a blog, contributed to by many of the leading figures in Irish food, and a comprehensive list of Irish recipes.